The Open-Winged Scorpion

THE INDIA LIST

ABUL BASHAR

The Open-Winged Scorpion
and Other Stories

TRANSLATED BY EPSITA HALDER

WITH SUNANDINI BANERJEE

LONDON NEW YORK CALCUTTA

Seagull Books, 2021

First published in English translation by Seagull Books, 2021
Original texts © Abul Bashar
English translation © Epsita Halder, 2021
This compilation © Seagull Books, 2021

ISBN 978 0 8574 2 550 8

British Library Cataloguing-in-Publication Data
A catalogue record for this book is available from the British Library

Typeset by Seagull Books, Calcutta, India
Printed and bound by WordsWorth India, New Delhi, India

Contents

Abul Bashar's prose needs to be translated into English—the thought occurred to me with a jolt as I travelled back from his home, on a local train, straining against a gust of wind at the compartment door. Yes, the beauty of his magically unsettling prose and the complexity of his narratives were going to be difficult to render in equivalents drawn from an utterly different language. But it was necessary, especially now, in these times of commercial globalization and national chauvinism and the dangerous illusions they peddle with such persistence.

Why a writer as brilliant and powerful as Bashar has not yet been added to the ever-widening realm of English-translated *bhasha* literature may not be so hard to explain. Perhaps because of the hegemony of upper-caste and upper-class translators and publishers. Perhaps because his writing defies the stereotypes that the elite, urban translators and publishers are used to encountering. The nuances of his delicate explorations of the Islamic moorings underlying the shadowy fringes of mainstream Bengal's vernacular regions is perhaps one reason why Bashar has never enjoyed a wide readership even in Bangla. He has remained a niche, even if acclaimed, author.

The idea of translating Bashar grew stronger as I heard snatches of a song amid the chugs and the whistles. 'Flowers have bloomed on the alek creeper, they have petals of twenty-one forms.' These unmistakably *marfati* Sufi words came from a man beside me in his mid-fifties, clad in the traditional attire of the pious Bengali Muslim, complete with white skullcap and beard. Sijda, the mark from regular prostrations for the namaz, had imprinted upon his forehead a bluish shadow. When I asked him, he said the song was an Islamic ghazal, as essential part of the *waz* or sermon he presided over in the villages near a popular Sufi shrine.

Then I asked myself, did I know? Did I know anything about what he was saying? Possibly, my decision to translate Bashar's stories comes from this moment. As a humble step towards him. My co-traveller.

Bashar's work is replete with the creative complexity of Islam as it is practised in rural and suburban Bengal, where mosques and mazars exist side by side, both as doctrine and belief, bound by instructions or ecstatically free. Bashar writes intricately and intimately about this lived Islam. This is another reason why his work needs to be translated and read much more widely than it is—so that more and more people may discover and understand Islam as a *creative* force, where dogma and scriptural strictness are intertwined with the fluidity of faith and the rituals of supreme surrender.

Bashar was born in 1951 in a remote village in Murshidabad, West Bengal, a district surrounded by three rivers. The India–Bangladesh border is nearby and the mighty Ganga splits into two here and then flows on—as the Bhagirathi in India and as the Padma into Bangladesh. Bashar's home was located where the Padma began her eastward journey. Gusts of wind bellow over the expanse of those silt lands. The type and texture of the soil changes every few miles, giving rise to different landscapes. Those who live there are weighed down with the constraints of a hard life. Sometimes those lives snap, unable to bear the burdens any more. Or unravel slowly, like the edges of the riverbank that crumble and dissolve in the floods.

But those lands are filled with stories too. Culled from the Qur'an and the *hadis* and held close in memory for generations. Stories remembered and retold, changed into myths and fables and lore. Bashar strings them like beads on the thread of *his* stories; they serve as markers of the human psyche's bondage, and as reminders of the absolute and irreducible freedom of a storyteller's imagination.

As a young man, Bashar started to write in the 1970s, when the feudal system began at last to loosen its hold over the land. This shift in power led to massive changes across all spheres of life in rural Bengal, some instantly, others slowly, over generations. At the same time, Bashar's Marxist convictions grew deeper and he also began to write poetry. He was 20 when, with a little money borrowed from his father, he published his first collection of poems. He was not born to privilege; in fact, his college education would have stopped for lack of resources had his startling literary talent not been noticed by one of his professors and his tuition fees waived. After he got his degree, he turned to writing short stories and novels in earnest.

His first novel, *Phulbou* (The Young Bride, 1987), shocked everyone with its ruthless exposure of Muslim domestic life. Its portrayal of intense religious emotion *and* sexual passion carried the unprepared reader into a realm of moral unease while its narrative craft engulfed them in a critical-affective enchantment. *Phulbou* won Bashar both critical acclaim and awards. In it, an old man, father of a son, marries a young woman and brings her home as his bride. In the world outside, the feudal system is crumbling, and land reforms are imminent. The old father and his young son represent the clash between the landed gentry and the new, free-thinking ideals of class struggle. Amid this simmers the unspeakable desire between the young bride and her stepson. Bashar's stories have always enmeshed religion and sexuality; it is almost his signature theme—as the plots grow more layered, the language grows more seductive. Bashar treats sexual desire as a primal force, the strongest of human emotions, and expresses it through unfamiliar and uncomfortable crises that either bring together conflicting characters or split them irreconcilably. Bashar, and/or his narrator, remains curiously dispassionate, even cruel, as he lets his characters endure tremendous pain, both physical and emotional. Even when the plot teeters towards a tragedy, his language erupts with poetic allure and sensuality.

In both his novels and short stories, Bashar engages with the nuances of party politics and political ideologies in order to reveal deep insights into urban life, gender, caste and even disability. He remains unique in his intertwining of rural themes and the mythological polemic of pre-Islamic and Islamic myths and stories from the Arab desert and concoction of folklores from the Mediterranean.

MYTHS AND STORIES FROM THE ARAB DESERT

In *Maru-swarga* (Desert-Heaven, 1991), another critically acclaimed novel, Bashar explores the Judaic (hi)stories of the Old Testament. This preoccupation is evident in some of his short stories too, as is his interest in Judaic and Christian myths in general. Myths that scattered in various directions across the desert, and mingled and merged with the dreams and languages and ethics of the multitudinous Islamic world. Myths that entered the local imagination through Islamic sermons, dancing their way into the imaginations of new generations through the oratory of the elders. Myths that mingled with the stories of Murshidabad, of the mangroves in lower Bengal. Myths that he wore as his mantle as he embarked upon his literary journey.

In the *hadis*, Jahura the prostitute scrabbled in the sand of the desert to find water for a dog dying of thirst. For this act of kindness, Allah made her the evening star—Johuratul Qubra (see 'Ruku Dewan'). A blind girl trafficked into prostitution, Ruku wanted to see the star rise in the evening sky. She prayed the namaz every day, to keep her soul pure with faith in Allah who showers his mercy even upon the prostitute and the dog, the two lowliest creatures according to the tenets of Islam. Bashar's world pulses with Arab-Islamic texts and contexts but never presents an ossified notion of religion. Names of the various namaz to ethical codes, references from the *hadis* and the Prophet's life—all these are interwoven with the lives of individuals and their community, a community not yet beaten by colonial modernity into an 'acceptable' shape. A community still forming or shattering along class, region and religious lines. Even along the conflict between heterodox and orthodox forms of that religion. Bashar's stories have references to local mystical practices; these are included not in order to present the traditional legacy of Sufism but, rather, the possibility of interpreting Islam creatively, the possibility of a critical stance against normative religiosity. In 'The Other Quilt', for example, he shows how orthodox Islam merges with local forms of economic oppression—one can 'own' or control a religion as easily as one can 'own' or control a cow or sacks of rice or, even, a woman.

When Islam is not a theme, it's a way of life, an individual's everyday experience and imagining. When the individual fails to formulate his own religiosity as the core of his being, it is often because he is trapped by intersectional marginalities—sectarian identities or ambiguities, depressed caste positions, or class and gender positions—crisscrossing within a bigger power structure.

Bashar brilliantly mines his land for narrative material—its complex and varied sectarian society, its caste-related power positions and anxieties, its multiple ritual imaginations, customs and values, its Islamic orthodoxy as well as its traces of Buddhist and Vaishnavite mysticism. All of Bashar's stories seem to hold up an 'unfamiliar'; they need to be reread several times for their numerous layers to be properly understood. It is astonishing to see how his retellings of mortal passions and follies from the remote corners of Bengal lay the foundation for a radical literary practice. Radical, yes, but in no way devaluing the preciousness of those lives nor sacrificing their historical-political significance upon the altar of poetic experimentations with form and language.

The tropes in Bashar's stories seem to be born from light, as though they were revelations. The sacred blood of Imam Husayn at the Battle of Karbala, the willingness of Prophet Ibrahim to sacrifice his son—these are both history and myth as well as a lived part of insignificant everyday. Somewhere, a Hindu girl falls in love with a Muslim boy (see 'Night Kohl'). Their unrequited love lives on in a tulsi plant, collected from the shrine of a Sufi pir by the girl's sister, abandoned by her husband and now grown old. She prays to the tulsi plant, bowing her head before it as she hears the muezzin begin his azan, a muezzin who was once that young boy in love. No, Bashar never advocates an easy syncretism; that would run the risk of becoming a dehistoricized remedy for the nationalist imaginings of Hindu–Muslim identity conflicts, especially in the secular-liberal discourses. He keeps things difficult, because life is difficult. He shows the inability of prevalent discourses, including that of the Communist Party of India, to grasp the emotions that are integral to religious identities, emotions that are all too often flattened in the name of 'class'. Bashar shows us a world where a man may be ostracized simply for having a hairless chest (see 'Simar'). It remains a puzzle whether monstrosity is innate to man or whether he is made into a monster under the pressure of religious imaginations. While many of his characters seem to be doomed, Bashar never fails to show us the tremendous beauty that lies within the heart of destruction. Bashar is rarely critical of his characters; instead, the reader is invited to experience their lack of choice, their various daily oppressions; their crushing compulsions; and their occasional exultant liberations, their triumphs of will. Bashar's narratives combine piety and subjectivity in a way far more complex than the pitting of religious oppression against secular liberal agency.

One cannot but shudder, wracked with both pain and aesthetic joy, at the intermingling of folk Islamic belief and narrative device which results in a father dressing up as as the horse of Imam Husayn, in the battle of Karbala, in order to pray for the return of his dead child (See 'The Road'). When the man who cares for his horse more than he seems to care for his children beats the animal, the reader flinches at the pain yet feels the intense love binding man and beast. It is remarkable how Bashar creates such avant-garde forms of prose, how he explores and radicalizes his themes without imposing any urban-middle-class perspectives or judgements on them.

Unique narrative estrangements occur also because of Bashar's use of desire, both spoken and unspoken, a desire that stains the ever-expanding visceral spaces of sound and texture and colour, light and taste and words. A horse comes back to its rider in the forest and nuzzles him awake (see 'Simar'), and the rider wakes up with a start, remembering the breath and touch of the bride he killed on his wedding night. The frisson of awe at a scorpion's multicoloured wings can signify a young girl's apprehension about her inevitable sexual violation (see 'The Open-Winged Scorpion'). A father's unnatural lust to taste the first crop of the season may be symbolic of his sexual desire to impregnate his wife in close proximity of his college-going son (see 'Sister').

Bashar's stories are also stories of the land, vivid commentaries on the political and economic nuances of land. Cows and goods are trafficked; powerless human beings with meagre or no means caught in the web of a smuggling economy. Anyone may be a part of this nexus of money and power, folk performers, grooms and goons. Bashar is their chronicler, the keeper of their histories, the recorder of their experiences, no matter how distant and unfamiliar their home and their land.

Bashar had once said that in order to better craft his narratives, he had even internalized the structure of Hindustani classical music. Even though, in life, he makes no difference between *classical* music and 'Bollywood classical' music. Bashar can indeed play with form but that is not why he writes. He writes to tell a story. He writes to take the reader on a journey to a distant land, to people who may seem different to us but who, in the end, are not.

The stories collected and translated here are a part of that journey. They explore a few unfamiliar themes and rarely seen signposts on the Bengali literary landscape. The writer is courageous. So must the journeying reader be.

Ruku Dewan

Let me tell you that folktale today. Ruku Dewan said these words and glanced at Putu alias Kabir, her illegitimate son from Hindu-babu. Though she was blind, her eyes were a charming translucent brown. Beautiful she was, impossible to look into her eyes and know they cannot see. And impossible for you to know that she was a prostitute. Ruku Dewan, after coming to this red-light area, became Rukmini Dasi. In this infamous quarter, she was the most beautiful seller of sensuality. Even though there was no light in her eyes.

She had light in her eyes till the age of seven. That was when Ruku lived with her parents in Masjid Para, Village Tirail Joyari, District Rajshahi. Masjid Para was a pious neighbourhood. Immersed in praying namaz five times a day, a three-fold life of religion and poverty, two folds poverty and one fold religion. But religion was no less strong than poverty. Nothing but roza-namaz-fitra-jamat-Muharram-akikah-tasbih-summah-haram-halal-kalma-surma-nur-farishta-zaqat-zurmana-huri-husna-keyamat-korma-shirni-khorma-Mecca-Medina-murda-hasar-gor-doya-darud-jennat-jahannam-talaq-niqah-janeja-sijda to live for.

Every so often the women of Masjid Para got talaq. And one or two teenage girls simply vanished. Then, one day, another story unfolded: a group of Urdu-speaking elders came to the village in search of young brides; their own land had a shortage. Some of the local boys helped guide them here and there. Jumma Shaikh was one of those elders.

Ruku's father Barkati Dewan said: 'I want a Bengali groom for my girl.' Ruku was fourteen then. The light in her eyes had slowly gone out. She was learning the stand-ups and sit-downs of namaz by holding onto her mother's body, and the words of the kalma by having them read out to her. She was married off to Jumma.

Jumma was the pimp of the Urdu-speaking bride-hunters. He brought the beautiful-blind bride Ruku from that side of the Padma river to this side, to Harudanga. Enjoyed her body for about a month. Then they set off for Swarupganj. To Dhanai, the trader, in whose courtyard Jumma gave Ruku talaq and bartered her for cattle. Dhanai was a cow trader and a pimp. He kept Ruku as his wife for two months, then dispatched her to Daspara. To the prostitutes' quarters. From there Ruku was trafficked to Kolkata by one Hindi-Urdu-speaking Badruh Keora. It was the time of the 1968 famine. People were starving. Whatever food was available in the market could only be fed to the dogs. Still, they were celebrating Bakri Eid. Ruku was bartered again. This time, for a tiffin-box full of qurbani meat and rice. Tempting her with the promise of more meat and more rice, Badruh brought her to Sonagachhi.

Ruku of Masjid Para became Rukmini Dasi of Sonagacchi. She was kept by Taraknath Naha. Putu was his illegitimate son.

Ma, Ruku, would tell her son, Putu, a folktale.

A rare sight indeed. A beautiful blind prostitute performs the Maghrib, the evening namaz. When she is done, she will tell Putu the tale of a star. She will take her son to the terrace of the prostitutes' house and say, 'See, Putu, can you see? Look up at the sky.'

These words will be heard by Kaloshona too. She too will look up to the sky.

'That star is in the sky,' Ruku used to say, 'If you can spot the star, Allah will bless you. He will pardon all the hundred sins of this life. Kaloshona, can you see it? This star used to shine in the evening sky of Masjid Para. If its light touches the eyes of the blind, the blind can see again. My mother used to say so. That star is surely there. My mother was not able to show it to me but I want to show it you, Putu. Johura is its name. The light of the Arabian Desert.'

The other prostitutes would drift up to the terrace. They too would search for the desert star. Johura.

'If I could get back my sight, I would like to go back to Masjid Para, Putu. There is no light in Kolkata. O Kalotogor, is there a customer on the street? Has Johura appeared in the sky?'

The narrator of this story is a sannyasi. As a child, he was known as Putu among the prostitutes. This is the story of his mother, a beautiful, blind Muslim prostitute who wanted her Hindu son to be a sannyasi. Because, when it was time to admit Putu to school, Satyananda Maharaj the sannyasi had given by way of alms his name as the boy's father on the admission form. After receiving this sublime gift, Ruku Dewan began to dream that, one day, her son would be the one to cleanse all her sins.

Ruku educated her son up to MA. How that Putu became Sambuddha Sannyasi without being tainted by the hell he lived in is another history. The reader will not get to know that here. Here, the reader will be told an Arabian folktale preserved in Ruku's memory. It can be found here, in this biographical tale 'Ruku Dewan' by Kabir Dewan, that is, Putu.

Kabir, or Sambuddha Sannyasi, continues: 'With what intense devotion, Ma would tell me this tale. Let me tell it you today.

'"Look, look at the sky. What do you see? A star. Johuratul Qubra. Even into the pen of sin, Allah can pour the ink of virtue." This tale would fill Ma with a bliss as vast as the seven heavens. Her face would glow with infinite wonder, with endless joy. I must have been ten or twelve. From before, much before, she had been telling me this tale.

'Perhaps Ma's sense of sin was endless because she was a pious Muslim. She read the Fajar namaz before the first rays of the sun and the Maghrib as soon as the sun set. She'd bathe with scented soap just before the Fajar.'

Sambuddh can still recall that beautiful scent. Ma was so particular that she would not let even her son touch the jaynamaz, the prayer mat.

'Taraknath refused to acknowledge his paternity. Once I'd called him Father, and he slapped me: "Father? Who's father?"'

'Life is such that Ma, from Masjid Para, blind Ma, fourteen-year-old Ruku, wife of Jumma Shaikh, later bartered for cattle, brought along with her only a star.

'That childhood cannot be forgotten. Ma wanted to see that star through other's eyes. Through Kaloshona's eyes, through Kalotogor's eyes. Through Putu's eyes. When Maghrib went away, many of the prostitutes gathered on the terrace of their house of sin to gaze at that wondrous star. Maghrib comes and goes on horseback. Only then does Johura appear in the sky.'

A child and a flock of prostitutes look for Johuratul Qubra in the evening sky. Why?

How virtous a deed had Johura performed, then?

A deed of great virtue. But a trivial deed too. That people do not do out of negligence.

'One day, Johura saw, in the middle of desert, a rather bedraggled young dog dying of thirst. There was not another human in sight.

'Often, Ma would stop at this point in the story. Somebody would call out: "You've got a customer at your post, Rukmini. Come down."

'A lamppost in front of Ramdas' laundry—that was Ma's post. Ma would hold onto that post and wait for a customer. Kaloshona would hold her hand and lead her to it, help her stand against it.

'If a customer came, Ma clutched a corner of his shirt and followed him up the stairs. Often a customer would disappear without paying the blind prostitute her full price. So she began to call for the others, to count the money before the man could leave. Some of the women would be irritated by this. Only Kaloshona, if she was free, would come and quickly do the counting.

'Taraknath said, "Putu has learnt his numbers—surely he can count his mother's money for her. After all, he'll be your pimp sooner or later. So no need to worry, Rukmini."

'The day I went up to count Ma's money, Ma was angry. And devastated. "Don't you dare, Putu! Don't you dare touch even one note of this sinful money! You're not your mother's pimp, Putu. You're a student. You have to pass your BA and MA. Become a learned sannyasi. Go, study. If you're bored, you can count the stars in the sky. But never this sinful money."'

Everybody has a favourite tale. Ruku of fourteen, from Masjid Para of Tirail Joyari, en route to Swarupganj Daspara, brought to Sonagachhi during the famine of 1968 . . . and her tale of Johura, the desert star. Ruku got married by reading the Qur'anic kalma, and her journey followed a predestined path.

The story started all over again on the terrace. A true story.

Noon in the Arabian desert. Waves of mirage water rippling away into the sandy horizon. The sight of which only made you more thirsty.

Johura was coming back alone from the desert market.

'O Khwaja Khijir,' she said, 'O angel of water. Please don't confound anyone with your illusions, O Friend. O Merciful One, please guide the wretched traveller down the path to ab-e-zamzam. I have never uttered the name of Khoda, but now I am praying to you, O Lord—please lend an ear to this prostitute. I have heard that you are wise, that you enlighten everybody so that they can tell that what shines in the distance is not real water. That only the water of zamzam is real water, O Khwaja.'

Talking to herself, the fallen woman Johura travels from one horizon to another. She has no one in the world. In the desert harems, such lonely prostitutes are not an exception.

Johura had been forced to survive by selling her body. So lowly a prostitute was she that there would never be a place for her in any royal harem. Nor in the sun temple. She'd never be eligible to be offered to the Sun God. An ordinary prostitute. Not even taught to utter the name of Allah. She used to think that she was so fallen that she had lost the right to call that name.

She had no place in society. Nor could she do anything for anybody. Nor was there enough water in this desert for her to drown herself and her burden of sins. In any case, she was sure that when she died she would be sent down to the worst of hells.

It was the eyes of such a woman that suddenly fell upon the dog, dying of thirst, just a little older than a puppy. It had not realized the trickery of the desert mirages, O Khwaja!

'Oh, such a little thing. He'll die of thirst, lying like this in the middle of the desert. A wordless creature, come out all this way chasing a mirage, and now without the strength to move, parched and panting!'

A wave of compassion seemed to ripple through her chest. She began to search for water. She looked at the dog, and then this way and that. But there was no water to be seen. She ran from one well to another only to find them all dead and dry.

She ran one or two yards away from the dog, and then ran back to him.

No. There was no water anywhere. This time she began running three-three yards away, in every direction. Until suddenly she found the ab-e-zamzam, a well full of water, real water. As if the sacred water of zamzam, glistening at its bottom.

A mere three yards away—properly measured, perhaps only two and a half yards away—from water and you're all set to die!

Standing at the edge of the well, she leant over and looked at the water. There it was, but so deep down. Rippling like the waves of compassion in Johura's heart. As clear as the eyes of Khwaja Khijir. But how to get some of it up for the poor creature?

'Why did you come here to die?' Johura said to the dog as she stood there beside the well. Then, as she lifted her eyes to the sky, she felt she would begin to cry. Never before had she really prayed to Khoda. Coming from the worst of hells, with a soul most sinful, with a body so polluted, a heart grown as hard as stone in this unforgiving world, such a person could have no Khoda. Could have no god, could utter no sacred name.

That day that fallen woman prayed to Allah for the first time, 'O Merciful One, O One without Compare, Father of the World. This insignificant creature is your creation too. A stray dog. Save him, O Lord.'

This call, this heart-wrenching cry was heard by Allah, the god of the desert, and in an instant she was granted the spark of an idea. Her mind said to her, 'There must be a way! We must get water, Johura, however we can!'

'Water! Water! Holy water. A palmful of water. A wordless creature. Whom does he have in this world! He is dying of thirst, O Lord of the Seven Heavens!'

Calling on Allah and muttering to herself, Johura started to tear her clothes to strips. Thus a rope of cloth was made. Then she tied one shoe to one end of that rope and dipped it into the depths of the well.

Water! Water! Up came a shoe-full of water.

Johura carried that water with utmost care and tipped it into the mouth of the dying dog. The water of compassion. The water of mercy. The tears of the desert god. As cool as Johura's heart.

The water brought the dog back to life.

'See,' Johura said to the revived animal, 'you're a wretched creature and I'm a fallen woman. Come, let's live, together.'

The dog attached itself to Johura and began to live with her in the desert's red-light area. That wordless creature knew no one but Johura, its mistress the prostitute Johura.

Then one day, Johura died in an accident.

The dog had grown old by then.

He sniffed and sniffed at his mistress' body and finally understood that she was dead. Then he looked up at the desert sky and filled it with a mournful cry. Howled, over and over, that Johura was dead. An isolated route, under the shadow of a date tree, away from the market—that's where Johura died. Neither the tree nor the whirling wind of the desert could tell the dog how to bury her. The leaves merely swayed in the dry wind, bowed their heads. Dusk fell. Nobody came to search for Johura. Because she had nobody. No pimp. No friends. Her body just lay there in the dust.

The dog kept vigil over his dead mistress. This is true. Because only dogs can keep vigil like that. In truth, it too had nowhere else to go. An old dog, who would want him now? And most importantly, how could he leave his mistress and go? So, he stayed where he was, sitting beside Johura.

Suddenly he saw an extraordinary glow emanating from her body as it slowly dissolved into a ball of light. Slowly, before his eyes, she was gone. The ball of light rose into the air, then above the earth and upward into the sky. Then it turned into a star and grew still in the firmament, shining bright.

In the western sky, the star shone bright beside the moon. The dog gazed up at the star and began to walk towards the distant mountains.

Then, at one point, he too disappeared somewhere behind them. Never to be seen again on the desert sands.

Kabir is also walking, gazing at a star in the sky. He is remembering his Ma. Ma is no more. Ma died of tuberculosis.

Suddenly he turns and finds a black dog following him.

The mosque in Masjidpara is echoing with the sound of the evening azan.

As the dog stops behind him, Putu alias Kabir whispers, 'Come, Messiah.'

And they keep on walking.

Translated with Chandrani Chatterjee

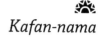

Kafan-nama

Chinibas' grandson Sudhan sits in the boat and prays the Asar, the afternoon namaz. Unlike his wayward Dada and Nana, Sudhan is a devout man. Sudhan's Dada, his paternal grandfather, was Ojha Chinibas Barui, in the Sunderbans, the owner of a betel-leaf orchard as well as a bishahari ojha. On Sudhan's mother's side, his Nana was Hakem Dhanilal Baidya—dispensing herbs and talismans. And Sudhan's father Madhubas sold fotash jal—bottled soda water.

Like a man's fortune rises and falls, so too do the islands of the Sunderbans delta. When they rise from the depths, one can no longer recognize the island or the man. But if a man is mauled by a tiger, his face changes even more than those islands. That is what happened to Madhubas. His face remained his face no more.

Madhubas of Madhukhali—what a bitter name! The mauling from the tiger had turned his face grotesque. In shame and pain, Madhubas hid his face in a giant kochu leaf and lay under the jack-fruit tree. But the orchard in which the tiger pounced and ripped a life to shreds, that orchard withered away. What to do now?

The human countenance is Khoda's handiwork. Mauled by the paws of the mangrove-maneater, the beauty of the beautiful is destroyed. Even if you cry for a hundred years, that beauty will never return. Now what was needed was a tolerable face. Behind the veil of the giant kochu leaf, such a face was created by a light-eyed suley-mani baidya, Baba Gaffur.

Somewhat restored by Gaffur, Madhubas set off for Dhamua station to start life as a soda-water seller. But he soon realized that the customers were repulsed by his face. It frightened the children. Made the men move away. One child was so frightened, it began to scream. To soothe its fears and stop its wails, the mother pushed a milk-filled breast into its mouth and hastily patted its back. Even the problem-solving fakir halted and hesitated before he felt brave enough to reach out for a bottle of Pocha Company Fotash. Water from Panchanan, alias, Pocha. Hence the name.

Madhubas Barui thought about killing himself. He just couldn't figure out where to hide his face. Standing by the Matla river, he stared at its frothing currents and thought about how to keep selling his soda water. Finally, he gave that up, and became *assistant* to a boatman. But how much could he earn by helping row a boat to and fro? He had to give that up too. Besides, there too the faces of the passengers would pale at the sight of his scars.

Madhu has roamed the streets from Canning Market to Mograhat, the fotash bottles hanging from his shoulders. Thought about selling fish but couldn't muster up the courage. For two months he bought eggs from the Ramchandrapur poultry farms and then sat with his basket at Sonarpur station. But 'Oh God!' the *doctor's wife* exclaimed, 'This one's been eaten by a tiger! How can we buy anything from him! Horrible, Kaninika—let's go!'

Madhu tried many things. Even being a pimp at the red-light area of Ghutiyari Sharif, for the smallest-*sized* prostitute. But he soon realized she had tubercolosis. Then he tried selling paniphal at the local market—but failed at that too. After that his mind simply stopped working. Who knows what happened then but one day Madhu went to Lal Mohammad Cloth House in Canning Market and asked to buy his own kafan.

'Run out of kafan cloth, Madhu,' Lal-miyan said, 'let me get a fresh bale first. How can I give you cloth for the dead from the cloth of the living?'

The boat floats on the Padma. There's been a light shower, but now the clouds have moved away and a rainbow has drawn patterns across a rippling white sky. As if across the Padma the Khoda has built a hanging bridge. The river flows under the rainbow, down beneath its very middle and off all the way into the horizon. The boat moves in a westerly direction—if you offer sijda now, you feel the boat will sail straight to Kaaba. It is important, thus, that one keep track of east and west. Paban Guri grips tight the side of the boat. Of course, Sudhan was the first—overwhelmed by the rainbow—to ever imagine Kaaba Sharif in the heart of the river.

Madhubas, Sudhan's father, used to imagine differently. A widow draped in white—he'd see her every now and then in his mind's eye, soon after the tiger struck him. Fotash didn't work, paniphal didn't work, pimping for a feeble prostitute with tubercolosis didn't work, rowing the boat didn't work—nothing filled the belly. So Madhubas became a sinner. And soon after, he began to be haunted by the widow.

Bodi-maulana of Mogra said, 'Bonbibi, goddess of tigers, is giving you nightmares, Madhu! Stop going to the widow quarters in Gosaba, a bad wind's eating you up.'

'Why, huzur-maulana?'

'When a tiger attacks, humans lose their minds. When Dakshin Rai strikes, husbands die. Women turn into widows. The sight of widows everywhere puzzles the mind, makes it sick. What to do, Madhu—best you go away. Leave this tiger island and move up the bank of the Padma, up to where the boatmen live. Things are in place. You have been a doctor. Now you can become a boatman.'

'Yes.'

'Your surname will now be Maktabi. I will present you before the assembly and then send you to Harudanga. If you become warden at the maktab there, you'll earn respect. But always keep a kafan with you, Madhubas. If you keep a kafan, Khoda will pardon all your sins. Think about it—a livelihood from the Padma's guri fish. What is wrong with that?'

Madhubas thought about it, and said, 'Yes.'

That a man is always carrying his kafan, his shroud, and his ijer, his loose trousers—that is strange indeed. Dispatching him to the Harudanga maktab, Bodi- maulana set off to meet the assembly.

But Madhubas cannot read even a single verse from the Qur'an. He can only utter an 'Allahak' and then lie flat on the ground in reverence. His tongue is strangely stiff, his memory so weak. So not the warden but the ugly sweeper, that's all he could become. He would sweep the maktab before the Fajar at dawn and the Maghrib at dusk. To wash away the smell of fish, he'd bathe with Sunlight soap. Then one day, who knows why, that maktab suddenly shut down. Madhubas came away to a mosque in Sheikhpara and took shelter there. His kafan came with him.

Bodi-maulana had said, 'Dakshin Rai struck a deadly blow—that's why Madhu's lost his wits, lost his senses. Thinks he's a sinner. So: "Keep the kafan close and safe, want to wear it in my grave." '

Madhubas was not good at scripture but his faith was strong—the light of Khoda would flood his face like the tidal waters of the Padma. The kafan stayed with him, proof of a powerful deathwish. And Madhubas kept seeing the widow in white, and the terrible tigress pouncing in the orchard. A frightened Madhubas, rowing his boat in the heart of the Padma, would raise his hands to Khoda and murmur, 'Make me beautiful, O Compassionate One.'

A guri fish leapt up from the water, and, scattering rays of light, told him: 'You are still beautiful, Madhubas. Keep saying Allahak. Keep on saying his name.'

Today, from the other side of sandbank, a learned angel-like man took a ride on the boat. He was, in fact, the one who had given the money for this boat. Half of Madhubas' life lay mortgaged in that man's pockets. Just the sight of him used to set Madhubas' heart thudding.

Sudhan, Madhubas' son, and now the boatman, could never fathom this man's arrogance. He wasn't a moneylender, after all—he'd just donated a boat to a boatman, and hadn't wanted the money back. He'd said he was happy with some fish every and then, to roast with brinjals and eat.

Mir's voice when he spoke was full of mystery. 'You're just like your father, Sudhan,' he said, 'Praying the namaz on the water—just like him. Praying to the Kaaba on the water. Faith—that's the real thing. Faith can bring close to you that which a knowledge of the scriptures still keeps afar. Do you know how far? From Madhukhali in the Sunderbans to Madhurkul in Murshidabad—from the Lower Bengal mangroves all the way up to the midlands.

'Bodi-maulana brought your father to the midlands to teach him the scriptures, to make him a teacher at the maktab. But that beggar's thick tongue allowed nothing but Allahak.

'Yes, Mir-baba.'

'So what could the poor fellow do! Madhubas packed his kafan and set afloat on the river in this boat. But he could barely swim. He feared the water as much as he feared the tigers. He'd say, "Not on this water land do I want to die, my baba—I want to die on shore."

'I was a teacher, and quite keen on religion. I gave this boat to Madhubas. Throwing his net into the water, he stood there, his waist bent, and asked me, "Do my river prayers truly reach Kaaba?"

'If you plug your nose with scented cotton, son—will a boatman stop smelling of fish? "They say the dust of prayer on a man's forehead makes him truly beautiful. If Khoda wills, does one's beauty return? It doesn't? How sad!"

'Yes,' said Sudhan, his head low as he pulled at the oar.

'Madhubas would sit in this boat,' Mir continued, 'his kafan held close to his chest, staring at the other side, a man in exile. One day, throwing his net, he fell into the water—that's it. All that remained in the boat was the kafan. To be buried on land is a matter of luck. But he had none such. People came to me, they said, "The boat's still afloat, still carrying the kafan. What to do, Mir-sahib?"'

'What did you do, Mir-baba?'

'What could I do? I own the boat. So I said, "Bring it back." People said, "But what about the kafan?" After much thought, I said, "Call Bodi-maulana." Bodi came and said, "Masterji, you keep the kafan. Can a kafan be thrown away?" I asked, "Why did you make Madhu carry it about, Bodi-miyan? You—a learned man?"

'Bodi lowered his voice and proceeded to tell me a strange story indeed.

"Huzur, Allah knows that Madhubas' mother was a widow without marriage. Tauba Midda worked in Chinibas' orchard. Midda seduced her with the promise of marriage and made her pregnant. Then one day, when Midda went to the forest to collect honey, he was killed by Dakshin Rai . . . Then Chinibas, his voice trembling with grief, declared that Shafitan, the woman, be kept in the widow quarters in his name. In truth, Chinibas is not Madhubas' kin at all.

"Shafitan stayed in the widow quarters with her newborn, Madhubas. When Madhu grew up, he started working in Chinibas' orchard and was given Chinibas' name, Barui. In truth, Madhubas is fruit of Midda and Shafitan's sin—he's a bastard.

"After the tiger's terrible blow, poor Madhubas came to me, his voice choked with tears, "Midda's tiger has destroyed me too, Maulanasàheb. Are there no instructions on how to save me?" I said, "There is. There always are." '

The story brings tears to the eyes of twenty-two-year-old Sudhan; they roll down his face and fall into the waters of the Padma. In the homeless abode of the Padma, at this afternoon hour of prayer, the water whispers La ilaha illallah.

If this is the story of his father, who is Sudhan then?

II

Mir was on his way back from Rajapur. Wearing an Ismail-brand lungi, a white kurta and carrying a beautiful cloth bag on his shoulder. The islands were rising in the heart of summer's Padma. From one of them, Sudhan rowed a small, thatched boat to shore. Mir got off. Suddenly Sudhan discovered that Mir-baba had forgotten his bag in the boat. What is in the bag? A comb, a round mirror and a diary. And wrapped in a white cloth, a pocket-sized Qur'an-sharif. How extraordinary! This white cloth must surely be that kafan?!

Sudhan thinks that Mir-baba has left it behind on purpose. What has Mir-baba written in it? Setting aside the comb and mirror and Qur'an and kafan, Sudhan opens the diary and begins to read:

'This kafan is not mine. If it is not mine, then why do I carry this burden, O Malik ul-maut, Master of Death? Like a wise animal, I can now see Death. Elephants certainly, but tigers too and even the tiniest of cats can see Death. That's why they choose their place to die, then wait for Death to arrive and then slowly, like its shadow, become one with it. Early man could see Death—but we cannot. Because we sin. Jesus carried his own crucifix. Prophet Ismail told his father, Prophet Ibrahim, "Dear Father, Tie a cloth over your eyes and offer me as sacrifice. Then your pain will not be so great." My pain, alas, does not fade away at all.

'Madhubas covered his face and shoulders with a gamchha when he went fishing. In shame and disgrace. His wife Jahira was beautiful, and didn't want to give her body to that ugly husband. She used to work in my cow shed. One day, I took her as my mistress. The sin was mutual. When Madhubas came to know of this, he drowned himself in the waters of the Padma. His mother Shafitan had been kept by Chinibas. His wife Jahira was kept by Mir . . .

'So what is this kafan for? Dear Khoda! Every night, Madhubas comes asking for it back. He says, "You are dreaming, Mir-jada, now wake up. Give me back my ijar. If you can't, then give me the kafan that is mine. Don't give the rest if you don't want to. But give me the kafan. Wake up, master." '

Sudhan reads and a tremor racks his body. He lifts his eyes to the sky. His classmate Bilal used to say that his Nana-ji, the teacher-merchant Mir Sultan Hossein, was an engraver. Inscribing poems and proverbs in praise of Allah-Rasul on plates and bowls and wells and homes and graves. On handkerchiefs too. He'd been published in Islamic newspapers and magazines. He used to write a diary. Keen on religion, he was an angel-like man . . .

Sudhan brought his wandering eyes back to the page:

'The kafan is the attire of the grave. The poor can only manage the sheet. Or the ijer. For them, any one is enough. Before dressing it in its final attire, the dead body must be bathed. Usually, a female bathes a female and a male bathes a male. But a wife can bathe her husband, can touch the dead husband's secret organs, and this is a wonder indeed. The bathing of the dead is an extraordinary poetry. In this matter, I have a wish, a desire. I am writing it down so that the community may *permit* it.

'My wife is ugly. But Madhubas' widow Jahira is beautiful, an absolute flame. For her, I have erected a tower of desire in my body. Madhu-fisherman was ugly. Is it acceptable that an ugly man's wife be so beautiful? My wish is that Jahira will bathe my dead body.'

Sudhan cannot read the diary any more. Tying the boat to the bank, he goes to Bodi-maulana. His heart and soul have run dry. His body is caked with salt from the Padma; his eyes sting from the briny waters of the Matla and the Bidyadhari.

As soon as he laid eyes on him, Bodi-maulana knew. 'Mir has returned the father's kafan to the son,' he said without preamble, 'Read the burial rites, then throw it into the river, Sudhan. Your father's asking for it. And listen, on the first day of Ashadh, Mir and your widowed mother will get married. To drive away this island's spell of death, this is what has been decided. Don't be sad. Go. Oh and listen, listen—death at back and marriage in front, such this is the riddle of this land.'

'Yes, maulana-saheb. The burial rites are for a grave on land. But now it will be performed for a grave in the water.'

Sudhan shook with silent grief.

'Before she marries,' said Bodi-maulana, 'Jahira your mother has asked for a plate full of jackfruit. Mir has said, "All right. Once the jackfruit ripens, the marriage will follow." On the first of Ashadh, the first day of the monsoon. The stump of the jackfruit tree will be covered by kochu leaves again, my son.

> *From the earth did We*
> *Create you, and into it*
> *Shall We return you,*
> *And from it shall We*
> *Bring you out once again.*

Your father Madhubas had so badly wanted to die on land.'

On the first of Ashadh, Sudhan immerses the kafan into the waters of the Padma. He is aware of the burial rites. This earth is your body, now we bury you in this earth, in this earthly grave. We will bring you up again, again you shall live . . . But the words get stuck in his throat. He cannot even cry.

But then Sudhan sees one of his father's hands come out of water and draw the kafan into the Padma. And then, deep underwater, it is fought over by a tiger and a tigress. The rain begins to fall, like a sheet of white cloth. Sudhan whispers, 'Bring you out once again—wake up, Father!'

Underwater, the tigers are feasting on a live dead body.

Translated with Chandrani Chatterjee

The Open-Winged Scorpion

Other than my sister and I, nobody had ever seen such an insect. An entirely new kind of creature. Black like a tamarind seed, with a thousand legs the colour of sundried mango, as dry and hard as a giant crab shell, crackling almost; three-quarters of an arm's length. On either side of its body, wings nearly as large as a human palm.

As large as a human palm, and spread open like a peacock's tail, half-moon in shape, open wide. What a pair of wings!

No butterfly on earth has been blessed with such multicoloured and beautiful wings, so incredible are they. As though the creature carries upon them all the world's grace, all its supreme beauties, so vibrant are they. The spot seems aglow. The giant stump of a felled palm tree, still rooted to the earth, covered with grass, and on it sitting still that terrifyingly beautiful creature.

At first, it seemed the glitter from a heap of gold. At the next instant, like diamonds. Then like a cluster of precious gems. Shining like priceless jewels, gleaming metals. Its wings gently throbbing. Maybe in anger, maybe pleasure.

Slowly, slowly, it inched its way down the stump and then towards the ridge that ran along the paddy field. My sister and I were frozen to the spot. Too scared to move even a foot.

Birds, when they fly, first half-straighten their wings and then slowly open them wide. But this creature did not fly—it just opened its wings a little and crawled down off the stump.

The stump looked as if it had been burnt. Often, the cowherd would make a bush fire on the stump to roast berries. Was the burn mark from such a fire?— we could not tell. It seemed more as though a fire had been blazing there just now, that creature's body a living flame. A black-hearted bonfire.

Was the creature a reptile or an insect? Was the creature a bird? Moving along the ridge, as if burning the grass beneath it. As if scorching on either side of the ridge the Dudh Thor paddy stalks, heavy with ripened grain, as if withering them away.

I am going with my sister—to help coax her way back to her in-laws'. Never had we imagined that we would come across such an open-winged scorpion on the way!

Our customs are different. If the in-laws refuse to take back our daughter, we must coax and cajole until they do; we cannot afford to take offence. Even if a husband does not feed his wife, she must still be taken back to him. Things like this happen often in our lives. Twice already I have taken my sister, Ashmantara Begum, back to her in-laws'. The father-in-law hemmed and hawed, didn't want her back, but I forced them to keep her. First for seven days, then for forty. Then my sister ran away to us.

Sagardighi Nuncha is our village. We are poor. I am a primary-schoolmaster, my character modelled on a maulavi *pattern*. I sport a curly black beard, shave my moustache. Sometimes, like Uttam Kumar, I go entirely clean-shaven. Being whimsical about beards gives one a bad name, prevents people from trusting you. Following the Faraizi pattern, I have shoulder-length hair, though there is a tiny bald patch on my crown. My name is Bichhadi Mir. My good name is Mir Nasiruddin.

I write poetry. I also recite various Islamic texts. Use attar. Wrap around my shoulders a scarf printed with the Kaaba-sharif. Not all the time, though, only sometimes, only for formal gatherings, only for readings and soirees. That's when I use the attar too. Attar is expensive.

I recite in the courtyards of householders, once in a while, that too at night. Sometimes compose ghazals and then sing them at religious gatherings. Such as:

My heart is a myna bird
In its cage it will not stay
To golden Medina
It keeps on flying away

This is one of my most popular ghazals. At every gathering, they insist I sing this song. But now, let me tell you about a sin of mine. These days I no longer read the texts. Over the course of those night-long singsong recitals, I entered into an immoral relationship with a married woman. My bhabi, or sister-in-law, the mistress of a reputable household.

Disaster would have been inevitable had I kept up our contact for much longer. Not for her perhaps, but certainly for me. Intoxicated by the rhythm of my readings, she'd sway before me like a black cobra. Her face would glow, her eyes would glitter, her lips swell with desire.

It was this sister of mine who saved my reputation from ruin. I kept thinking, if I go further with Dwina-bhabi . . . if I taste the pleasure of her body . . . no doubt her soul will be satisfied. But if I enjoy another man's wife, then my sister too can be enjoyed by who knows how many men. It's been a year now that Ashmantara's husband has refused her, has left her here with us.

Father is no more—there's only me. I have a job from the MLA quota. I was an active member of the Jama'at—the secretary of its local office. Then the MLA said I should give that up—that party won't help ensure your future, better you have a job, he said—and made me a Marxist. Gave me this job. If they are given jobs, no doubt many will turn Marxist like me.

The ridge seems to be crackling with fire from the scorpion moving along it. Its wings throbbing, swelling. Maybe in anger, maybe pleasure.

One still and silent afternoon, I sat with Dwina-bhabi in her empty drawing room and said: 'Hold Mecca in one hand. Medina in the other. In your mind. If I can tell you which is which, we'll be friends. Come on—hold them in your fists, then.'

Such peals of laughter. Such pleasurable posturing.

She was quite surprised. But gesturing confidently, she said, 'You must know magic.'

Then, in a voice that combined awe and impatience, she asked: 'Can you cast a spell too?'

I said nothing.

I have a friend, studying Bengali (Hons) in college, his name is Masiul, he's a poet. His poems are published in well-known magazines and journals. I'm very close to him. I played Mecca–Medina with him once too. He'd sent off a poem to the most renowned Bengali weekly and wanted to know if they would publish it.

I said, 'Let's play Mecca–Medina, and we'll know.'

'How?' he asked, laughing.

'Where will you put your poem—in Mecca or Medina? Keep it where you wish. Hold it in your fist.' He kept it in Medina, in his left fist. 'It's in Medina,' I said. 'You're under the sign of Medina now. It *will* be printed.' And it was.

Since then he too was convinced that I knew magic.

I must know magic—or how did I get a job in this terrible age of unemployment! How?

Extra beauty, extra poverty, excessive religiosity—these are my only possessions. My sister and I are both extremely beautiful. These days, it is said that poor people have vast families. Their numbers are uncountable, their votes innumerable. One job per family earns one thousand thank-you votes. In the last election, when we voted for the Muslim League, sadly our one thousand votes were wasted—the League candidate could not recover even his deposit! Then, we joined the Jama'at.

'Bhaiya! It's all burning!' screamed Ashmantara and clutched at my panjabi. She looked at the scorched tree stump, at the withered rice fields, at her destiny. In one hand she held Mecca, in another Medina. But she couldn't bring herself to ask me, 'Tell me—which is where? Tell me—how long I will have to sneak across these fields to go and live with my husband? Surma for my eyes, the bindi for my forehead, the red alta for my feet, my check-check *bodice*, my star-patterned saree, my palanquin, my Harempur—where are they, bhaiya, how far?'

Dumping is a bad word. Harsh to the ear. Insulting. But without this word, how can I narrate the story of my sister's fate? Her journey to her husband's, as though Sakuntala's journey to *her* husband.

A baby goat had come running up to Ashmantara, wagging it's little tail. This baby goat would hop about, hop about and then roll over and then fall down and then bleat for help. Try to drink its mother's milk but miss the teat and bump against her belly instead. It was Ashmantara who would guide its mouth to the milk. When we stepped down into our courtyard just before daybreak, a darkness-dispelling wind was blowing and the morning star shone brightly. The baby goat came running from its mother, and began to pull at the hem of Ashmantara's saree. It was a girl, and so young that my sister had not had time to name it. Why it woke up, and why it pulled at her saree—did it know that Ashmantara was going away to her husband?

The creature moves on and on—be it insect or reptile. Its wings are thin and meshed, like a bat's, but more colourful than a rainbow, ablaze with a thousand colours. The slightest ripple and they seem to sparkle with fire.

'These fields belong to my father-in-law—all 22 bighas. They'll all be destroyed, burnt to ash. So why should I bother to go, Allahak?' asked my sister, her voice choked with despair.

She no longer wanted to go to Harempur. We had left before the sun rose and would reach just as it set. The day will have been spent on the road.

The sun was setting in the west. We did not know how far we'd travelled to reach the 22-bigha boundary in Harempur mauza that marked the estate of Ashor Biswas, my sister's father-in-law.

On the ridge's western corner stood a pair of fig trees, so calm and cool their shade. Something there, shone like a tiger-skin. It was a tiger-skin-clad Kali! A bright-red tongue. A fearsome scimitar raised high in one hand. One leg rested against the tree trunk, the other on the ground. The anklets glittered.

A Kali impersonator! A rare sight in these parts. From the other end of Bati-Kholsheypur, the bahurupis cross the river and come to this side.

The winged creature had turned the corner on the ridge and was drawing closer and closer to the Kali. 'Run!' my sister and I screamed. Startled, the impersonator brought down its leg from against the tree. Jhom—its anklets jingled, though on the whole it did not seem very perturbed by the crawling creature.

'Who are you?' I asked.

'From Munger,' it said.

The voice had a ring to it—the bahurupi was a woman! 'Why have you come so far?'

'I didn't come—I was brought. I make bombs, rifles, muskets. Train the women here to make weapons. Play a bahurupi too. Been brought here by the MLA. My man and I.'

'Did you see that insect?'

'Insect! What insect! Everybody is an insect here—where are the humans? Only insects everywhere. CPM insect, Congress insect, Fugitive Party insect. Insects raping—thhoo!'

'Fugitive Party?'

'The party that gives birth to insects, turns them into fugitives. Say MOO!'

We were frightened. Frightened of the scorpion, frightened of the Kali. Frightened, we cried, 'Moo.'

'Go,' the bahurupi said, 'Moo—and keep going. There's the checkpost head. Five rupees for every cow. Say moo—hide in the herd, and get through.'

Hide in the herd? Why is there a checkpost? Confused, the pair of us stood there, unable to move.

'Why aren't you going?' the bahurupi repeated, 'Go! If Ata-babu asks you, say you're coming from Hiron.'

And she stamped a foot on the ground. Jhom—the anklets jingled. Kalis like this we'd sometimes seen, standing as a scarecrow in the middle of the paddy field. Now as we looked more sharply at its feet, we discovered that it was not a woman but after all a man!

Leaning against the pair of fig trees, that figure sends a chill down our spine—a swatch of raggedy tiger-skin and the rest covered in black umbrella cloth; its lolling red tongue; its upraised scimitar; its two extra Chamunda arms at the back, swinging up and down, wobbling like *springs*; anklets jhom-jhoming with every step . . .

The man, his anklets clashing and clanging, that bahurupi man, that man from Munger, he told us a story. To this district's border, to its outermost villages, on the other side of Ganga Prasad, they come, this man and his wife, to teach the art of making bombs, making muskets. At first, they'd been invited by Nabi Mukhtar or some other infamous dacoit. Deep inside the jungle, in a vast trench, they built their bomb factory. Soon, guns from that factory flooded the nearby villages. Then, when the village gangs were armed, the political parties took them in. Here, even the housewives know how to make bombs. Rolling bidis was a livelihood, now so was making bombs. In the name of Bismillah, they make both bidis and bombs.

My sister Ashamantara made neither.

The bahurupi had spoken to us in a woman's voice. The fields around us seem to echo with her words.

Ashmantara had a soft heart. She loved to dream.

'I'm wearing Dwina-bhabi's clothes, bhaiya. Her *snow* on my face. She said, "Put these on. And our son-in-law will love you again." The granary's being filled with rice—the 22 bighas are reeling from the smell of ripe grain! Alam the trader told me so. But that Kali will ruin me, bhaiya! That insect will chew me up alive! Will I not be saved, O Merciful One, O Prophet! Saviour of the Poor, Protector of the Skies!'

'Hush, Ashmantara. Hush!'

Still frightened, we spoke only in whispers.

Suddenly the bahurupi began rushing about, scimitar in one hand and a bird-shooing bamboo pole in the other. Then we realized that it was scaring away the grain-eating birds. Khot-khotaash! went the bamboo pole and the bahurupi's two extra arms flapped behind it like sails.

The clacking of the bamboo pole enrages the scorpion, and it starts to swell its wings. Then suddenly it shoots up one foot above the field. Then two feet. Then three feet.

A dirt track emerges from the forests of Bihar, and, cutting through this district of West Bengal, wends its way to the other side of the border, to Bangladesh. Along this track travel shipments of smuggled goods, trafficked cows. Both the police and the BSF—Border Security Force—are involved. Along this track come weapons-expert Bihari men and bomb-making women. Like the nyada insects on every sheaf of paddy, politics begets insects on the arse of every village. But how Khoda-Halshahana creates such winged insects, no one can tell.

The scorpion was wriggling and writhing, crumbling and shrinking, its wings crushing, as if they would tear apart. Slithering and sliding.

'Don't be afraid,' I told my sister. 'When the rice grows ripe, man's heart fills with desire. Curdling tight with love. Melting as soft as butter. The village then becomes the garden of paradise.'

Ashmantara giggled at this explanation, then fell silent with fear. Then the open-winged scorpion rose even higher into the sky, coiled its tailtip near its mouth, almost forming a circle, then cracked it back sharply like a spring, then whistled out a note. Then rose higher and higher, whistling melodiously. And a thousand colours played across the sky.

We left the field and began to walk along the road. Is the checkpost this way? Suddenly we heard someone walking behind us.

'I'm now playing Forward. Used to be CP in college. No more. Will Bush go or Saddam—who knows, who cares. Our village Hariharpara is now Chambal—dacoits everywhere! Jiziya to be paid too! And now a new party—called Faw-Baw-Cong—in Harempur!'

Startled, we turned and saw the bahurupi. And Ashamantara finally recognized who it really was—it was her brother-in-law Ziaul, pet name Pinu.

'It's you, Pinu?' she asked, astonished.

'Yes. Ata-MLA's party has asked for four muskets. It's the tax. Jiziya. We have to pay. They've already taken seven cows right in front of our eyes, right out of our cowshed. Elder brother said, "Let's start

a gun factory, then musket-basket—we'll give whatever they want."
Told me to fetch you.'

'But you didn't come to get me!'

'I would have. But you're too beautiful, Bhabi. The head musketeer from Bhagalpur, Munger—he visits our house every night. I
don't want his eyes to fall on you.'

'Who?'

'VIP. From the most influential party in Bhagalpur. Bhikupada
Gunahgar. Come, this way.'

And Pinu the bahurupi sped off, disappeared into the horizon,
leaving us behind. It was clear that he had no interest in bringing
his sister-in-law back. In fact, he was not at all pleased that we were
coming home.

Suddenly we were surrounded by herds of cows. Three tall men
in turbans were goading them on. Swept up with them, we had no
choice but to move on. Whenever we tried to speak, a cow would
moo and drown our words.

Suddenly, we saw Ata-MLA's checkpost. Beneath a pair of neem
trees, a bamboo gate—a long bamboo pole, lying across the road at
waist height, balanced on a stump at either end. Ata-MLA sat on a
stool near one stump.

Since we could not speak to each other, we had begun counting
the cows. I counted forty-eight—tall and short, red and brown, black
and white, etc., etc. Forty-eight in all. A cloud of dust. Dust on my
beard. Dust on Ashmantara's well-oiled hair.

Ata chews betel. Pokes his teeth with a toothpick. Smokes 555.
Once upon a time, in lungi and full-sleeved shirt, and clutching an
umbrella, he went from door to door, collecting for the party fund.
He'd been a son of the soil, then. Revolution on his lips. The land's
special patrolman, then. Now he's the captain of the 420 cavalry, the
custodian of cartridges.

Once, he gave satiric speeches, mimicking the nasal voice of Congressman Ajoy Mukherjee. Once, applause had been his signature tune. That Ata was now a tool-man. He'd lost his chair on stage.

'Stop!' Ata roared.

We stopped. The cows stopped too. Ata began to count the cows. Ata was an *Eight-pass*, knew his tables, learnt his numbers upto a hundred. Once a believer in the powers of literacy, a lover of learning, Ata had been the torch-bearer, leading the way to the light . . . That Ata was now a 'tota', a party parrot with nothing to lose but his shackles. That Ata now counted the cows, tugging at the ropes round every their necks and noses.

His counting done, Ata went back to his stool, sat down and began to write in his notebook. Counted the numbers on his fingers. A one-eyed comrade held open the umbrella to shield Ata's face from the sun.

Dear sister, these are the evil Dajjals, the false prophets. Who ride in on donkey-back when the world is about to end. The donkey's right eye is blind as is the Dajjal's left. Two huge sacks hang on either side of the donkey—one side is Heaven, the other Hell. Masih the Dajjal, the Prophet says, will carry Socialism in one sack and Fascism in the other. He will have kaf-fereth written on his forehead. Though the world will be flooded with literacy, and the light of learning will shine in every home, no one will be able to read that word. All the pages of all the true books will have been erased. All the homes of Bengal will be homes only to pornography. Under the covers of Sarat Chandra's works, the Bengalis will relish *sex guides*.

What will happen then, Ashmantara? How will you go to your husband's house then? The acid river will wash away the red alta borders on your feet. Drops of dew will wipe away the surma in your eyes. Dust will engulf twilight.

The donkey will have a small square box on its head. Across its screen of glass will float scenes from Heaven. Torments from Hell.

Oil will rise from the earth like smoke, rise up into the air. Up in the sky, sky-sentinel Azazel will create an open-winged scorpion. What will happen then, Ashmantara?

The evil Dajjal will say, Come. I know the shortcut to Heaven. Look at the glass, see the terrorized cities, the raped villages. I'll put one of you into the sack of Socialism—come. He will go to Hell, to Ata-MLA's check-post. The other I'll put into the sack of Fascism, that one will live under the flag of liberal democracy, in the wasteland of an employment bureau. Doomed to weave on the loom of unemployment benefits. He'll be called The Chosen One. He'll wear a cap lined with peacock feathers. Wave a fan at Kapalitola's double police station. His title will be *Home Guard*. We'll never be entirely certain whether he will or will not become a rapist. A hundred shiuli flowers will bloom across our land then, Ashmantara. And one kick from the donkey's foot will bring down the Berlin Wall.

'Two hundred and fifty,' Ata finally said, as he finshed counting. 'Fifty cows *into* five.'

'Fifty! What kind of counting is this, master! Are you counting the ones in the wombs too?'

'No.'

'Then from where did you get fifty?'

'See, Nabi Mukhtar's chap is standing there—I can't argue. I never make a mistake with my counting.'

'Whatever you say.'

'Hey, BDO, you, Kana Nafra—count again.'

Kana, the one-eyed umbrella-holder's nickname was BDO. Closing the umbrella, he proceeded to use it to recount the cows, one by one.

'Hey, no tricks, Ashor Biswas' daughter-in-law,' BDO roars at Ashmantara, 'Stand straight, don't fidget.' And he counted both of us too.

'I'm the wife of a weak man, Ata-babu,' pleaded Ashmantara. 'I am helpess, like sorrow-loving Sakina. Alias Ashmantara. You are my in-laws' kin, Tota-bhai.'

'Tota? Who's Tota?'

'You're the nephew of our hurricane-holding head of the panchayat! You have succeeded in getting us onto the *dry dole* list, the wage-labour master list. You are an LC member!'

'What member?'

'You are our own caliph. You are the bird of paradise. The phoenix of fire.'

'Oh!'

'Yes, you are. We won't be able to pay five rupees per head, master. I want to buy dolls from the village market. Buy candy sticks.'

'BDO, hurry up and count!' Ata-MLA roared, 'Need you to *counter.* Need a counter-revolution. Won't give me money but buy dolls instead! Dolls? Candy sticks? No skin on your body, yet taking the name of God?!!'

'After all, I am the Biswas' daughter-in-law. And they are *general body* members.'

Ata-MLA seethed with rage! This girl was defaming his party! 'Damn farmer's wife—spurting English! What wife are you? Whose wife? Does your husband feed you? Does he? Then why do you creep in like a beggar? Why doesn't he keep you? You must have some fault. That's why you sneak back in. Sneak back through the fields. Why? Tell me!'

'Here,' I said and gave him two fresh five-rupee notes out of my pocket. Then I pulled my sister's hand. 'Come, Ashmantara.'

Suddenly, Ata uttered a terrifyingly cruel sentence. 'Your sister will have to go to Munger! Sold your sister's beauty and bagged a job! Shame on you!'

We were borne along by the flood of cattle. But oh what a blow, Allah! Where to keep this agony!

A different MLA got me the job from his *quota*. But even that is now stained with sin. We are poor, we are not meant to be beautiful. Our lives are unseemly lives.

My sister buys dolls and candy sticks—is that seemly? For whom does she buy them? For the son of her co-wife. Vast-bodied. Dark, freckled face. Missing four teeth, and the rest held together with brass wires. Her mug's not really ugly as it is manly. A huge mole on her chin, bristling with a clump of hair. A devout lady, she lived a life of tasbih—a life of rolling her prayer beads—her heart drunk on the teachings of the Qur'an. Thus was Zikira, Ashmantara's co-wife.

Zikira believed that with a strike of his fist the Prophet had broken the moon in two. Since then, the moon carries the imprint of his palm. That's how the moon got her marks, signs of her fairness being split in two. Zikira holds her son in her lap and shows him rockets in the night sky. Sputnik, twinkling like a star. Ashmantara gives a piece of candy to the boy. Zikira snatches it from his fingers and throws it away.

The two of us stood in front of the red-brick Biswas house. The herd of cows went off towards the Padma river, towards Bangladesh, a huge cloud of dust floating after them. Above the threshold of the Biswas house was engraved 'Welcome'. And a hammer and a sickle and a star.

Then we heard the evening azan. At once, my sister covered her head with the end of her saree. One must not keep one's head bare when the azan calls.

My sister's eyes grew moist. I was her father, her mother, her sibling—everything. I knew why she was sad. Hesitant and full of doubt, desiring and fearful and yearning—her heart was atremble with all these.

'Will there be place for me, bhaiya?' she asked. 'Look, I hold Mecca and Medina in my fists again. In one is the candy stick, my home. The doll in the other, my land, my future. Whom to keep where, bhaiya? Tell me, won't you, how to hold what?'

Ashmantara burst into tears. 'Welcome'. The sickle-hammer-star party, the Faw-Baw-Cong party, they are calling. Her musket-wielding, other-women-loving husband is calling. Munger-Bhagalpur is calling too.

I knew what was going to happen to my sister. I knew what the poor thing held in which fist.

Zikira threw away the candy. My sister had to seek out a little corner in that symbol-engraved comrade-house to dwell in. When her husband sits to eat, she rushes to cool him with a palm-leaf fan. Ashor's son Hashor. Hashor means roz-e-hashar. Means kayamat, Day of Judgement. People tremble at the name. Ashmantara's heartbird shrinks at the name. She rushes to fan him during a powercut. The husband is a strong man, he sprawls rather than sits at his food, his hirsute body swelling with every bite, his hair rippling like a lion's mane. When he eats, his son lies on his lap and sucks on a candy stick. Plays. Sometimes the father feeds the son a little ball of rice and fish.

When Ashmantara tries to fan him, he stretches out his left arm, sticks out a finger and stops her—as if he were stopping a bus on the street.

Ashmantara's face darkens with humiliation. This time when she returned she had made up her mind to never leave, never go back again. At the crossroads of daybreak, she told her namaz-reading step-grandfather sitting on his mat that this was the last time she was leaving her father's home. She would never return.

After rinsing his mouth, the husband wipes his mouth on his lungi. Then spreads his palm for some mouth freshener. When Ahmantara gives him some, he throws it to the floor.

'Why do you act like this, son of Biswas?'

'Because you have faults.'

'What faults?'

'Can't tell. Female faults. You're a houri, a trick of the light. You've got a jinn with you. A woman who grows more beautiful each day, more young each day—she is evil, she's got the fairy fault. Or . . . can't tell . . .'

'Why did you marry me, then?'

'You cast a spell on me. The fairy fault ensnared me. He who lies with you spoils his sperm. It's the *time* of war. Vultures fly in the sky. I need strength, need courage. The jinn has loved you, corrupted you.'

A *jet* plane speeds across the sky. The angels in their wooden clogs pace from one star to another. Jackals howl at the temple of Olabibi, goddess of plague. At the temple of Saturn, five cow-smugglers offer incense smoke and fire. And three baul women fill their lungs with deep draughts of cannabis.

Zikira was praying the midnight namaz. She sat on her prayer mat near one column. Counted her tasbih and stared hard at another column. Beside which sat an utterly still Ashmantara.

Zikira saw an angel. Suddenly, she rolled up her prayer mat and sprang to her feet. Lunged at Ashmantara and tore off her clothes, Dwina-bhabi's clothes.

The clogs walk on, from one star to another.

My sister is naked. Mecca in one fist, Medina in the other.

In the distance, on the river, a boat floats past. A dot of light. Outside the moonlight is blinding. On that boat, years ago, Hashor had brought home his bride Ashmantara. Down the desert's centre, down the parting in its hair, flows the Forat river.

My sister is a spinner of silk strands.

Grabbing the naked Ashmanatara by her hair, Zikira hurls her at the closed door of her husband's room. My sister, like an animal, claws at the door all night. But the door does not open.

My friend Masiul had written a poem:

The galaxy the Milky Way
On which walk shoes of gold
The red star sinks in the river
In the heart of the thatched boat fireflies glow
Such void such emptiness
On this riven earth
On the water, the boatman cries
And the tears of Medina fill his eyes
Such moonlight such a night—

The galaxy the Milky Way

Mecca in one hand, Medina in the other
Across the face of the desert
The Simoom threatens to blow
Such void such emptiness
Sakina, Sakina
Has spun handloom, has set flight to Buraq
Such a night such moonlight

The red star sinks in the river
In the heart of the village huts fireflies glow
On that path walks the golden iguana
The galaxy the Milky Way

In that Milky Way, from one star to another, leaps the open-winged scorpion.

My eyes fill with tears.

Outside, a sharp, sky-splitting sound as two bombs explode. Ata-MLA's political party arrive on donkey-back. Munger donkeys. The men shout 'Inquilab Zindabad!' Long Live Revolution! Shout for their party's unity over and above their rifts and clefts. Then come to a halt in the Biswas courtyard.

Very calmly, three gun-toting Dajjals put forth their simple request: 'We'll lie beside your woman tonight, Hashor Ali. Ready the room.'

In an outer room, Zikira laid a beautiful bed. 'Welcome.' Hashor smiled at the visitors. Three men entered the room, dragging my sister along. Tortured her all night. Two left at dawn. One stayed back. He had fallen asleep.

Outside the closed door, near the threshold, the husband stayed awake, smoking bidi after bidi.

'Awake?' he asked me in a whisper, 'Brother-in-law?'

My mouth was gagged. My body tied to the berry tree in the courtyard. I am a primary-schoolmaster. My character modelled on a maulavi *pattern*. In the Jama'at once, now a Marxist. I have seen a scorpion, a scorpion that has wings. Nobody has seen it but my sister and I.

The third man had fallen asleep beside Ashmantara. The glow of the bidi had fallen asleep too, outside the door. Then my sister came out and latched the door. She thought that at least this man would be punished. That the villagers would come running at her call. So she ran from door to door. Wake up, insects! Wake up, beetles! Wake up, Halsahana! Wake up, Tafadar-baba! Wake up, Imam! Wake up, Iman! O Rasul-phupha! O Idrish-chacha! Maimon-mami! O Harun-bhai! Wake up, people! Wake up, Islam! Wake up, society!

Running from one street to another, calling from one door to another, my raped sister could bear it no more. Lifting her froth-flecked mouth to the sky, she cried in a voice gone hoarse with crying 'Wake up, O scorpion!'

Then, at daybreak, she went back to the room, and—how strange—fell asleep beside that man. Nobody answered her. No human. No beast. No bird. No one.

Light climbs in through the window. Makes the courtyard shine. The man wakes up and walks off to an LC meeting, the light smeared all over him.

Later in the day, they brought up to the Biswas courtyard a mound of slaughtered human flesh found on the ridge of the 22-bigha paddy fields. The body of the bahurupi Kali. My sister does not cry. She just stares at the body of her paddy-protecting brother-in-law, lying there in his shroud.

Then Bhikupada Gunahgar, alias Jumman Khan, the true musketeer from Munger, arrives during the burial, riding on a black pony. The VIP.

'Salaam aleikum hajire janab. Janaja-e-Islam. Bajrang, Bajrang. Faw-Baw-Cong, Faw-Baw-Cong, scorpion-shine on, bat-winged hooligan, comrade machine-gun, lunatic Arabic, Ababil quadrille, iya nafsi, iya nafsi, O Khoda, what will be?'

And the burial was done.

My sister sat there, leaning against a column. She spoke no word, made no sound. Bhikupada placed two muskets at the feet of a devastated Hashor. Jolted out of his reverie, Hashor's eyes began to shine. Like thunder, his grieving heart growled a time or two.

'Payment for the woman, brother Hashor.'

For the price of two muskets, Ashmantara was sold.

'Don't go, sister!' I cried out.

Like a mad woman, she held out her fists, 'Which one is Mecca, tell me, bhaiya? Which one Medina? Tell Masiul-bhai I have not been spoilt. Ask him not to cry about voids, about emptinesses. It was the jinns that ruined me. Those three—they were not human.'

Then she looked at Hashor, touched his feet in a salaam and said, 'Give me talaq. Let me go.'

The black pony trots along the dirt track. Ashmantara, dressed as a bride, is going to Munger. Blessed with the divine touch of jinns, she will learn to make bombs. Or be bought by a sheikh in Kuwait. One day her picture will be printed in the newspaper, and the sheikh will be captured in Bombay.

But then Ashmantara might say, 'He did not force himself upon me. I am his wife, married by the kalma oaths. I am an angel.'

The Other Quilt

One day in one month of Ashwin, Ruhul-fakir looked up at the sky, astonished. The last of the Ashwin storms had blown over the day before. Yet there was a strip of cloud that clung to the sky. Puzzled, Ruhul stood rooted to the spot. He had crossed the border, gone to the Kushtiya baul festival on *that* side, to sing the melodious kirtans from *this* side. The baul songs of *that* side lacked the kirtaniya flair but possessed a fakiri simplicity and a lucid lyricism. Such things had been spoken of at the festival. Many other things had been spoken of too, including those fakirs who sat on seats of power. Of how conservative those powerful men were, how evil-minded, how wickedly they deceived their disciples. All these things had been talked of at length. Wherever there is power, there is corruption.

Ruhul was not happy. He shivered in the wind still wet from yesterday's storm. On this silt-land, the wind's whip was a ferocious one. Looking up, he could see the thunder and the fire still seething in the heart of the cloud. Its anger had not been fully spent. Every now and then, a soft flash of lightning. The strip of cloud seemed indifferent but its heart was full of grief. Any moment now, it would burst into tears.

Ruhul was standing at the V point. Maulavi Mijan Ali was standing there too, his bicycle facing east. One wheel on that side, one wheel on this. One rim smeared with the mud of India, the other streaked with the soil of Bangladesh. In his mind, Ruhul could not but marvel at the glories of the British administration. Then he glanced at the maulavi's Karl Marx–type grizzly and stout shape. A black muffler wound round his head, a thick yellow khadi shawl wrapped round his body, he was quite an outlandish figure. Barefoot, his lungi had ridden high above one knee and his feet were covered in mud. The sticky silt-land mud had not fully dried even in the daylong sun. Suddenly, there was a crack in the throat of the cloud. Both men looked up at the sky. All this was Mijan-maulavi's land. The border had been drawn midway through it, although it was invisible to the naked eye. All that was visible of the demarcation were a few scattered pillars.

This was the V point. The border doesn't run straight. It wends and winds its way, rises and falls and here creates the shape of an English V. When you stood at the base of the V, then one wheel of your cycle was in Bangladesh, the other in India.

'Assalamu a'la manittaba' al-huda!' the maulavi finally greeted Ruhul.

Ruhul started. What kind of courtesy was this man of Allah showering him with? He could tell that it was a greeting, but only Allah knew what the words meant. Yet the sound of it was friendly, so that was good.

'Salaam, Maulavi-saheb,' responded Ruhul.

'Yes. Assalamu a'la manittaba' al-huda!' the maulavi intoned again. 'Did you go that side to sing, you tuneless fakir?'

'Yes, I did,' said Ruhul, indifferently. 'But I could not understand your Arabicana just now, dear maulavi.'

'Oh it was nothing, fakir-saheb, merely a greeting.'

'But I've never heard such a greeting before,' said Ruhul, a bit hurt.

'How would you? It's not a common greeting. Not many people know it. It is *special*, only for non-Muslims. Assaalo-aleikum can't be offered to them—that is kept only for the Muslims, only for us. So I greeted you with the other one. He who has walked only a part of the Hidayat way of life, not embraced Islam fully or been unable to— this greeting is for such a one.'

'Good for you,' replied Ruhul, 'We're not Muslims, after all, we fakirs. But that the Qur'an and the *hadis* have prescribed such great humiliation for us—I had no idea. Never mind. You greeted me properly, yes, but your lungi is above your knee—is that proper?'

'It's proper when I'm talking to a shit-eating fakir like you. So, where are you off to? To Harudanga—to Tonu's place? Really, that girl has such charm! And those charms have so many ploys and ruses! Sixteen charms for the wedded man but sixty-four for the loitering lover! Go, go. That girl, she moans as loud as that cloud in the sky. Floods one *aisle*, yet the other *aisle* runs dry. See for yourself, how she floats about and teases us.'

Ruhul looked up—it was truly an incredible sight. It had begun to rain. The sun shone golden in the western sky while rain gently fell on the eastern *aisle*. One cloud, that kept its rain-shadow curled above India at the same time as it poured its heart out on Bangladesh. Sometimes, it'd be the other way round. Ruhul's heart was overwhelmed with the wondrous variety of Nature's ways. See, how one half of the maulavi's fields were wet, yet the other stricken with arid astonishment!

But the maulavi's words, like molten lead, had speared and scorched Ruhul's heart. 'The Qur'an and the *hadis* are the property of your community only,' he thought, 'And you want to evict us fakirs from it. You utter Bismillah, we say Allah is in every seed. Man is born from seed, the world is aglow and abundant with seed. You can never comprehend its true meaning, you scripture-clutching maulavi! You've only seen us eating shit. How can I explain to you the wondrous workings of form and fluid and seed and soil! I too offer you your Assalamu a'la manittaba' al-huda. As far as I'm concerned, you're not a "true Muslim" either.'

But 'Let me sing a song for you,' is what he finally said out loud, 'I've brought it from the other side.' And plucking a tune on his dotara, Ruhul began to sing:

O Allah's so devout devotee
Whose lovestrings bind you so tightly?
One day only darkness you'll see
Your actions tell me so.
Owning money, owning land
Holding a beautiful woman's hand
With such bravado today you stand
On this only earth we know.

Maulavi Mijan Ali, bent low, had been trying to scrape off the mud from his feet. The fakir's song-retort and the humiliation it flung back at him now further darkened his already dark face. Such is the *style* of the fakirs. To sing their responses, to sing their scorn, to sing their complaints and their revolts. No dark patch on the human soul escapes their eye.

Why Tonu's life was subject to such disrespect—Ruhul knew that only too well. Of course, he did. And this insolent and angry maulavi—the fakirs know his type well too. Ruhul was young, and a B.Com–pass. And not at all unfamiliar with life's realities.

An angel on your either side
Making sure the rules you abide
But pen and paper in bundles tied
You have not kept with you.
You loved and lusted without any shame

You forgot our Allah's name
You forgot why on Earth you came.
What are we to do?

Singing his song, the fakir walked on towards the silt-land slum of Harudanga. Evening began to fall. The evening star twinkled softly in the cloudless sky.

Life on the silt-land near the border is impossible, incomprehensible. And life around the Harudanga slum—there it was especially challenging. Afflicted with such restlessness, such uncertainty. Let me tell you about it now.

Tonu races against time as she stitches her quilt. She wants to sew the last stitch before the fakir arrives. The fakir will stay for one night only—no more. There were many reasons why. The locals hate the fakirs. Especially the scripture-clutching insolent maulavis. They believe that the fakir songs scorn the Sunnis, and that the fakirs possess the evil eye.

An unbridgeable divide. But Tonu, in the shadow of that divide, had glimpsed the glory of another life. The restless silt-land life seeks the security and stability of mainland life. But where to find such land here, where in Shaikhpara, Budhidanga, Kaharpara or Harudanga? In the evening darkening into night, Tonu shielded with her palm the flickering flame of the lamp and stared out at the eastern horizon, at the vast open silt-land stretching away before her. A chilly wind was blowing. Who knows how the fakir was on this cold evening! He was supposed to be back tonight.

Far away, a dotara sang a note or two and then fell silent. But that was perhaps only her imagination. This is what happens, this body itself begins to sing like the dotara. This body-dotara of Tonu's is an incomparable example of feminine form and beauty. A woman is a well of beauty, Nilratan Gosain used to say. Just as the base of the dotara holds music, so too does the heart of that great formless void. But is this body any less? It is in the formless that the Divine dwells. How can that be so? The Divine is without conundrum while the body is conundrum itself. Without the body, there is neither beauty nor music. And the thirst for that body is the thirst of the baul. Baul means 'the mad man'. Tonu was waiting for her baul, her mad man to arrive.

She put the last stitch to the quilt. And the fakir's melodious dotara stopped at her door. Tonight, the darkness on the silt-land was dense. Tonu was afraid. The Sunnis of Kaharpara and Shaikhpara did not want Ruhul to stay with her. A fortnight ago, as Ruhul and she were crossing the river, boatman Kader-miyan's grim expression had conveyed to Tonu that the times were very bad indeed.

Tonu knew how bad the times were. Knew why the boatman's expression had darkened with ill intent. Was it because Tonu's free-dom shone in the rising sun of the east? Nobody knew. Perhaps it was only her imagination.

Earlier that evening, Mijan-maulavi had come on his bicycle to inspect the land. Then he'd threatened Tonu, then charged off towards the V. Why was he angry with her? Because she was Tanzina, nee Tonu Khatun, the wife of Hajmat Shaikh. His second wife. Every-one in Shaikhpara, from the householders to the tanga-wala, knew this. So don't you forget! A Muslim's wife doesn't prance about playing Radhika. The fakirs can come and go as they please but they are not part of our community, they are not one of us. Don't forget that, my girl. I see you've stopped your five-time namaz. If you miss one, you go to Hell for eighty huqbas. One huqba is eighty years. So, eighty huqbas is how many years? Eighty multiplied by eighty—that's how many!

As she listened to him, Tonu's lips twisted into a smile, a small line of defiance. Such threats had been thrown at her for a very long time. Her husband Hajmat Shaikh was from this side. His first wife had died just a few days ago. She'd swallowed poison because she could no longer endure Hajmat's lust and lechery. Just a few days ago, and Tonu had heard that Hajmat was on his way to marry a third time! A girl on that side. And, sure enough, that's exactly what Hajmat did—his third wife was a girl called Lehejaan who lived on that side of the border. (Hajmat's first wife had, in truth, been a bit mad.)

Such things were not a big deal on the silt-land. If you had a smuggling business, it was natural to have a wife on either side of the border. Clever people did just that. Because smuggling was their real occupation.

One man, but with two houses, one on either side of the V. The house with the four thatched roofs on that side, and the brick house on this side—they both belonged to one man. Hardly a house— more like a mud hut, a small room. On that side, in Hajmat's room, lay Lehejaan. Tonu was also from that side. To help with the smuggling, she had been brought to this side and ensconced in a new house built by Hajmat. After settling her on this side, Hajmat began to seduce Lehejaan on that.

Those who didn't have co-wives had mistresses. In the darkness of the night, some of these women helped carry sackfuls of clothing from one side to another. If one had a wife on either side, and if one could inform the BSF accordingly, then it was so much better, so much more convenient. 'Where are you going, Hajmat?' 'I have a wife that side, I have children.' 'Where are you going, Tonu-bibi?' 'To my husband. He hasn't left my co-wife for a week.'

Ruhul had been spellbound by these tales. Last year, a young fellow had explained all this to him. What had that fellow said? As soon as she remembers the words, Tonu's face grows red with shame. The truth was that Hajmat hardly came to her any more. That young fellow had said: 'You know, fakir, on that side, Tonu's husband has another household. So on this side poor Tonu lives alone. Hard to know about the hardships of life unless one knows Tonu. She *goes* that side only to sleep at night—get it?'

Then he'd chuckled a few times and continued: 'By day a slave on this side. By night, carrying over a load of goods only so that she can lie with her husband. Such are the wonders of life! Death dwells in the two arms of the V. One bullet from the military, that beloved bosom will be ripped to shreds—the head will lie in India, the body in Bangladesh. Like water on a kochu leaf—one touch and life is gone. But tell me, fakir, what are you doing in this land of frauds and fakes? Tonu is a wild woman, as wild as the silt-land. Yet when you sing, she shuts her eyes and weeps.'

That fellow's name was Sovan. Six months ago, he'd been shot dead by a military bullet. Every year, the BSF would lay a body or two across the V as proof of their hawk-eyed border vigil. Sovan had been part of this year's demonstration. But such things did not stop the silt-landers. The path from this side to that, the path of this hour and that—a border could not stop their lives. They do not acknowledge the border. The distance to the other side was least at the base of the V while the vigil at its greatest. One could only get by through extreme cunning or lavish bribery. Yet that's the very path they used for their smuggling.

There are more twists to this tale, but, in a nutshell, death roamed freely on those wings, loomed over them like a shadow. The people never knew on which side they should settle down. Marriages happened between this side and that. Plays and music programmes on this side always attracted an audience from that. A boy from that side came to the weekly market on this side and then went back in the evening—yes, such things happened too. Here, death was as restless as life, wandering freely from this side to that.

Tonu yearned for a bit of stable land—her own land which could be touched and held and cultivated. Not wet-land, not flood-land, not even the terrors of the unpredictable silt-land of the Padma. But land like the soul of the fakir. And perhaps something more.

Tonu could not remember how many things the fakir had told her. Such as: the flame that shone just above the heart. The fakir wanted to tell her everything about its light . . .

That fakir is back tonight. A fortnight after the full moon, in a darkness dense and deep. In Tonu's hand, the lamp flame trembles every now and then.

During Independence, when the British split Bengal in two, a funny song used to be played on the gramophone. Boatman Kader-miyan sang it often, even though he'd forgotten bits of it and simply added words and tunes of his own. The uncertainty of life that swelled up in that song can be heard even today. Oh my lord my lord my lord—Kader-miyaan would suddenly burst out singing but more in the manner of a scolding, more like the burst of a thunderclap:

> *Now you've got your freedom, son,*
> *A freedom that's*
> *Killing the poor*
> *Now, tell me, what to do?*
> *Where to breathe freely, me and you?*
> *Where do we live now, O my son?*
> *In Hindustan? Or in Pakistan?*

That song always made Tonu laugh, made her body roil with laughter, made her stuff one end of her saree in her mouth to stop her mirth . . . and then think about the wild women of the silt-lands, whose utterly dark lives were entirely without a place of rest. Made her remember her burden of little deaths, her nocturnal smuggling that had made her Hajmat's sex slave.

People here were all fakes and frauds, thieves and murderers. They killed in this land and fled to that. Lived there for a while. When the king of the country changed, then under the *guarantee* of traders–

moneylenders–politicians–smuggler mafia and village-heads, they came back to this side. Killed again for the moneylender, for the village-head. There was infighting too. The Hanafi and Faraizi fought all the time. How many times one should call for azan on Fridays, one or two; skullcaps, round or square; how to lay the body in a grave, on the back or sideways—they fought on and on.

Such fights led to charred houses, public disgrace, sometimes even beheadings. Then there were the political plots and ploys, another set of regular rituals. Black money was spent on gambling, people fought over it . . . Another man's wife woud be visited by a dark and lusting shape . . . Suddenly, at midnight, a woman screams in terror, 'Thief!' But it's no thief—only a primal naked shadow. Another round of beatings, thrashings . . . Tonu does not want to be a part of this life. It is only hunger that has somehow made it hers.

That old cracked record turns on and on:

In Hindustan? Or in Pakistan?
In Kaharpara? Or in Harudanga?
Or on that side entirely,
In Lehejaan's courtyard?
Where does life come to rest?

Tonu's sigh makes the lamp flame tremble. And just then the shadow of the baul falls across her courtyard.

'I am here, Tonu.'

'I heard your dotara hours ago, fakir-saheb. Sit. Have some soaked rice. I do not know how to truly serve. Will you teach me the prayer-rites from your religion? Your faith of love for all men?'

'I will, Tonu. But slowly. This rule of offering me soaked rice— do you mind it very much? I told you the last time I was here to keep some for me. The stomach is like a leather pouch. It will expand, if you let it. If you don't, it won't. I told you once—remember?'

'Of course, I do. I will learn by heart whatever you tell me,' Tonu said, smiling sweetly. Then, lamp in one hand, she rolled out a small mat on the veranda. 'I'll give you tea in a while. Then light a fire for you. You won't be able to bear the cold of this silt-land.'

Ruhul removed the cloth bag from his shoulders and sat down on the mat. Leant his dotara against a bamboo post. Tonu placed a tin pitcher of water near his feet. 'Shall I wash your feet now?'

'You are the wife of a Muslim,' Ruhul replied, 'The feet you would have washed, the feet you would have wiped dry with your hair, those feet are not yours any more. Your husband is not yours any more. I am a fakir. I want a woman who's truly free to be the one to wash my feet. Your husband had uttered the consent word for marriage, three times. Bound you thrice over. One thread-word has been torn, for he has uttered talaq once. The remaining two—those you tear yourself.'

Hajmat was Faraizi. He would give three talaqs over three months. The Faraizi *hadis* is not as easy as that of the Hanafis. The three talaqs do not happen at the same time. The three talaqs need three full moons. Perhaps because of this, divorce was rarer among the Faraizis. Their religious rules and codes were stricter.

Hajmat had uttered one talaq to teach Tonu a lesson. To tame her a bit.

But Tonu was not the type to be tamed. And ever since she'd met the fakir, she'd been gripped by a strange desire. What that desire was Hajmat could not quite tell. Her eyes were blank, they gave nothing away. Sometimes he thought his third marriage had made Tonu oddly desperate, reckless. She could cross the border unafraid of a bullet but she could not touch her husband's body, for Lehejaan had captured him. So Tonu had grown jealous. Maybe she felt humiliated too. Maybe that's why she'd grown desperate.

Hajmat could not share these thoughts with anyone. Not even with Mijan-maulavi.

'I won't give her a full talaq,' Hajmat had told the maulavi. 'I'll just scare her a bit, make her behave. These days there's reason for us to be scared too, what if she files a court case and asks for alimony? She's a fiery one, got her wits about her. And not entirely illiterate either. She went to high school too, for two years, in Tirail. Her father had no money for a better groom. That's the only reason why she agreed to be a co-wife. What desire makes her so restless, only that damn fakir knows.'

'I want a woman who's truly free to be the one to wash my feet . . . . The remaining two—those you tear yourself.' Fakir's words had welled up from a heart touched by deep contemplation. But they confused Tonu a little. Her husband was estranged from her, that was true. She had spent that year entirely on her own in Harudanga. And now, for for the last three months, Hajmat had been pestering Mijan-maulavi for the talaq. Hajmat's plan had been to keep her in Kaharpara, make her smuggle goods to and fro, then come to his embraces every night like a bitch in heat. When such a plan falls through, a man is bound to be furious. He wants to bite and rip to shreds, but doesn't know how, for Tonu refuses to come to him any more.

At the fakir's words, there stirred within Tonu the woman from the ancient age of man, the brave matriarch of yore, the forceful spirit of feminine freedom. Tonu did not know who she really was. But this much she knew—the fakir had given her strength.

Last year, the fakir crossed the border to the other side. On the way, he'd come to her and left behind a yellowish robe, a white dhoti and a scarf. 'Please wash them for me,' he'd said, 'Use this soda. It's not from a shop, but ash. I collect it from the brick kiln—there's no need to spend on soap.'

Tonu was astonished. 'The poor man's way is also the fakir's way,' he had replied, looking into her surprised eyes, 'We don't need much. Very little to live on, even less to be fulfilled and content. These are not empty words, Tonu-bibi. Oppressed, downtrodden, crushed into the earth, flattened by life itself, nameless and colourless—we have built this way of life as our very own. To gobble up life, to eat only one fistful but waste ten more, then to weep and wail about it—that's not our way. Khoda has said, "Inna aa-thaina kal kausar. I give you kausar, Water of Heaven." It is there in the Qur'an. Do you know what it means?'

'My mother was the daughter of a Rajshahi farmer, a Hindu,' Tonu said, 'She spent a lot of time with the fakirs. That created a rift between her and Baba. One day, Baba ate beef and became a Muslim. Soon after that Ma disappeared. Without the right man, the body's desire becomes a noose around one's neck. Since then, I have fallen too. Since then, I've also been lurching this way and that. My life, slowly strangled by the body's desire and the belly's hunger. I have become a thief for two fistfuls of rice.'

'I have gifted you kausar,' Ruhul replied, 'It's the water of heaven—drink it and you'll never feel hunger again. In the heart of kausar blooms the force to dispel hunger. And that joyful drink lies within this body itself. Only the fakir knows where, Tonu-bibi. That's why your mother was drawn to the fakirs, that's why you lost her. The maulavis may perform inna aa-thaina five times a day, but they do not know where kausar lies. I will try and find your Ma for you.'

Now the fakir brought out some photographs from his bag. 'Is this your mother? I think I may have found her.'

Holding an ektara. Singing. A middle-aged woman, prettily dressed in baul robes.

Tonu leans closer to look, and recognizes her mother. Ma, singing at a fair. Beside her, Ruhul.

Tonu had told Ruhul the story of her mother. Told him her name. 'If you could ask around, fakir-saheb,' she'd requested.

And here, here was Ma! Tonu picked up the photograph. 'Oh, how much torture she had to endure! They cast us out. Didn't let us draw water. Pressed my father to give her talaq, harassed him day and night. But Ma refused to surrender. Refused to leave the fakirs. Instead, one day, she chose to leave my father. Their separation took place amid so many tears. So many tears shed as their lives were torn apart.'

Tonu returned the photo with a sigh. 'Baba married again into a devout Muslim family. My stepmother was a pious woman. Prayed the namaz five times a day. Then I was married off—thrown into the deep, deep sea. I feel bad for my mother. She'd once come back to see Baba. But everyone attacked her. "I haven't come back to stay," she told them, "I'll go away. My faith is mine, your faith is yours. To practice violence is not in our faith—it says so in the Qur'an." '

'Yes, in the Surah Kafirun,' said Ruhul, 'You cannot apply force in matters of faith.'

'Then why do they torture others so? Even the fakirs—why cut off their limbs? You're here now, and I'm so scared. Of course, if you're starving no one spares you a glance. But when it comes to religion, how they huff and puff!'

'A parrot religion,' the fakir had said as they had talked of her parents last year, 'The Qur'an for reciting only, not for living by.'

'What are you saying, fakir-saheb?' Tonu had replied with a shiver, 'They'll kill you if they hear you!'

'I won't be the first fakir to be killed, Tonu. They have murdered us. Beaten us. But we have never raised our hand. An ektara or a dotara—this is all we have, all we hold. No fakir can hold a knife. Our song makes the mind grow tender, and the taste of kausar washes away all bloodlust from our veins.'

'Why won't they huff and puff!' the fakir said today, 'They are the majority. We are the few. They claim that the Muslims have seventy-two sects, seventy-two firqa. There's even a song about it, though I don't remember all the words.' The fakir holds his breath for a bit, then sings:

There are seventy-two firqa
We are from one of those najiha
Whose firqa has only a few
Think about it, you know it's true,
We are few, a few good men
Mansur the martyred lover is one of them,
Sing for him, remember him,
Read Alhamdulillah
Of those far-flung bees, Ruhul sings today

'There is the Surah Nahl in the Qur'an. We belong to that surah, that najiha. So, of course, they'll kill us. I have been coming to you, Tonu. I will always come to you. Don't you want to see your mother? Is it a sin to come to you and talk about her?'

The fakir had said today that he wanted a free woman to pour water on his feet and be happy. Not as an act of worship, like pouring milk on the Shivalinga. But as an act of surrender between humans.

Last year, while crossing the silt-land, this fakir had sung:

If you want to meet the man of gold
Seek first the mad man of the heart.

Was the man of gold sitting in front of her today, dreaming the dream of a free woman?

Setting the pitcher aside, Tonu went into the house.

Suddenly, a voice: 'Are you home, aunt? Your householder's sent a bit of curry. Keep it carefully and eat it at night with your rice.'

A boy, about fourteen, entered the courtyard, a thin shawl wrapped around him and a plate in his hands. Tonu came out of her room, lifted the flame to see his face and then took the covered dish from him. Back in her room, she lifted the cover—and gasped!

Quickly, she covered it again, then held a corner of her saree tightly across her mouth as though hushing up a terrible secret.

Then, rushing out, she shouted: 'Rosul, listen!'

Rosul had left, but came back into the courtyard at her call.

'What's the householder doing now?' Tonu asked.

'*Meeting*,' replied Rosul. 'They're talking about you. Mijan-maulavi's there too. They'll come to you in a bit. They'll decide about you. Your husband has forbid you from smuggling goods with the team. And you'll get another talaq tonight.'

The boy turned and left. 'Rosul saw Fakir here,' Tonu murmured to herself, 'They're fixing my punishment, having a *meeting*. By a whim of fate, Rosul is their spy. His eyes, so big with fear! Chhi!'

Only that last word, Chhi, fell upon Ruhul's ears. After washing his hands and feet, he had sat down before his plate and touched the glass of water to his forehead with an 'aleq', just as the Muslims start to eat with a 'Bismillah'. But just then he heard Tonu exclaim. Startled at the Chhi, he looked up from the glass, then looked down at it again. Took a sip. Said nothing.

Tonu thought that Rosul was Hajmat's spy. Hajmat thought he was Tonu's. The boy swung like a loom shuttle, pulled and tugged between them. How sweet his voice was. Tonu had been unsure at first about taking the curry. The sight of it had filled her with shame and weariness. Whenever such gifts came from Hajmat, it meant he'd come to spend the night with her. It could be a dish of vegetables, a *cream* or a *powder* or even a saree. At the very least, some coloured bangles. Everything, every thing, stained with shame. Preventing her from breaking free of this filthy life. Yet the thought of free-dom was frightening too. 'And you'll get another talaq tonight.' Those words, entangled and entwined with such distaste. Life seemed to be trembling like the shadow of the lamp that was busy scribbling shapes on the mud wall.

Tonu sat there, staring at the shapes.

The smuggling of sacks across the border—supervising it was Tonu's job. Rosul carried them the rest of the way on that side, delivered them to her householder. Rosul also carried money to and fro between husband and wife. She was paid per sack. Their relationship was more like that between a master and his slave. They were husband and wife only as far as their bodies were concerned. But the bodies could not, did not, speak. Music lies only in the curve of the dotara, that swell that was called *tonu* in the fakirs' tongue. A woman's body was like a dotara to the fakirs, hence their madness. While for the Sunni, that body was a naked fruit to which flocked swarms of blue-bottle flies just as they did to the fajli mangoes of Malda.

Thinking all this, Tonu let out a deep sigh.

Ruhul heard her. Looked up at her. Gulped down the rest of his water. Then said: 'I have never seen a wife-talaq with my own eyes. I guess I will today. I wonder what you'll look like when it happens. Only in this country can we have such public humiliations of women. Anyway, when will they come?'

'I don't know,' Tonu replied, her voice grim. Then she got up and began to gather firewood. She'd light a fire, then roast two rotis on the clay oven and fry some vegetables. But she couldn't stop thinking of that curry her householder had sent . . . she' made up her mind to just throw it away into the darkness somewhere.

'Come,' she called to the fakir, 'sit near the fire.'

'Why did you say chhi then, Tonu?' Ruhul asked. 'Did Rosul's words hurt you? One thread is torn already, Tonu. Are you scared?'

'Yes, I am. If they do something bad today? I won't be able to bear it if they dishonour you.'

Ruhul smiled faintly. 'When have they ever honoured a fakir? We don't want honour from them. We only want to be left alone. All the religions in the world— they are all imaginary. All made out of the smoke of blind passion. Reason has one religion. Other than the fakirs, all religions are scared of reason. Lalon said:

A Muslim is he if he is circumcised
But a Muslim woman—what is she to do?
A Brahman is he if he wears the sacred thread
But a Hindu woman—how can I tell you?

'No one has been able to tolerate these words, these words of reason. They never understood us when we said that Allah is not in *la ilaha*—Allah is in *illallah*. They thought we were making fun of them.' The fakir paused for a moment, then continued: 'As a result, their religions make no place for women. Only men. While we, we think of women as our path to prayer, to divine adoration. Without the companionship of Prakriti, the Feminine, our religion is futile. The attainment of the feminine *is* our religion. They have it in some *hadis* that woman is made out of man's left rib, out of a bit of curved bone. So it's useless to try and straighten her—a bent bone does not straighten. Rather than straighten her, give her talaq—that's much more sensible. It is a *hadis* instruction, so what is man to do? But aren't all the *hadis* written by men, written for men? At most a drop of sympathy or two for women, but no real respect. Unable to bear such disrespect, Lalon sang, "What is she to do?" It is the light of reason, Tonu, that gives flight to the mind, sets it free. That light should be lit by human beings. Leave this thieving life, Tonu—I've said this before too.'

He slowly put away the photgraphs, brought out a notebook from his bag and began to write by the light of the lamp. Tonu lit a jute stalk from the lamp and touched it to the pile of firewood in the courtyard. Then, setting a mud bowl on the clay oven, and before starting to make the rotis, she spread the embroidered quilt round the shoulders of the hunched-over-and-busily-writing fakir. 'I've lit the fire,' she said, 'Come, sit by it for a bit. And see, see how the quilt has turned out. This cold of the silt-lands killed my child, fakir-saheb. This cold scares me a lot.'

Ruhul's pen stopped at her words. Speechless, he stared at her. And just then Hajmat's team of smugglers burst into the courtyard.

Settled around the fire and began to talk loudly among themselves. Most of them were young boys; there were only two girls. Young things. All of them would cross the V at midnight, carrying their sacks. Sacks they now placed on the ground, and sat upon like stools.

Capping his pen, the fakir stepped off the veranda and into the courtyard.

It was just a mile's distance from Kaharpara on that side to Harudanga on this. Her husband was holding a *meeting on that side*. Mijan-maulavi was being its voice of reason, custodian of the Qur'an and *hadis*. Not a smuggler but a moneylender for sure. Grown quite rich from his two horse-drawn carriages. Imam at the masjid, now a *member* of the panchayat as well. What will happen when they come? He's sent word, I'm not to go tonight. He's sent curry . . .

Tonu could smell something rotten in all this.

Tonu had embroidered her life on the quilt. Her Kaharpara life. The forest around the village. The brick furnace. The vegetable creepers winding up the bamboo frame. She'd stitch-painted it all. A tree. A monitor lizard. Gleaming gold. The sight of it makes you shudder. There was the grey mongoose, the one that lived at the brick furnace. There was the black owl. And the tree, the one called Kalnagini. Its hood like that of a snake. Somehow it seemed even more frightening than a real snake.

The fakir sat with the quilt wrapped around him. The smuggling team stared at the fakir. And at the quilt. Some of them even felt a bit scared and unsure.

The fakir saw none of this.

Tonu, rolling out the rotis, looked up occasionally at the boys and girls. They had confused the fakir with the quilt. Their eyes were full of hate, they could not tell that it was only a quilt and not the fakir's skin. That the fakir was not the enemy. He was not a beast from the jungle, nor an owl or a cruel snake. He was but a simple man of faith.

That I have wrapped him in the quilt, Tonu thought, what does it mean? The fakir knows nothing about the life I'm entangled in. What I have placed on his shoulders—the poor man has no idea. Tonu's heart wept softly at these thoughts, seemed to grow empty and emptier still.

The night grew longer, hour by hour.

Suddenly, Hajmat and Mijan-maulavi arrived along with two crisp young men. The fakir did not know them but could tell at once that they were killers. He realized something terrible was about to happen. Tonu sensed it too. As soon as he walked in, Hajmat barked an order at one of the young smugglers: 'Better be off now. If you spend all night warming yourselves, when will you bring my goods? Tonu's not going tonight. Go.'

One of the young men recited in response:

Chest grows warm but back stays cool
By the fire sits which fool
Sack from one side carried to the other
India here, Bangla over the border

Yet, they seemed reluctant to leave. 'Come, let's go'—said no one. They all seemed to be basking in the glow of the rhyme. Slowly, the words sent a thrill pulsing through them. As though it had been a call to arms.

Tonu, poking the fire for the last batch of rotis, told them, 'Wait, Don't go right now. I'll serve fakir-saheb, then I'll come with you.'

Tonu couldn't help bursting out with her request. The fakir was alone, and the strength of his faith alone could not slay the fierce beast. Or, could it? If there was a drop of man in the beast, perhaps the beast could be killed. Around the fire hung an infinite veil of darkness. When the fire blazed stronger, the veil moved back an arm's length or two; when the fire lay low, the dark strode closer again. The dance of light and dark, like a Santhal dance, holding hands and touching waists and swaying . . . Tonu couldn't help thinking how strange it was.

The flames in her clay oven died out.

Mijan-maulavi had been staring at Ruhul. 'Let the boys listen to some songs before they go,' he said without shifting his gaze, 'It will lift their spirits. What, fakir-saheb, won't you sing us a song? Music is sin, but I find your songs full of sensual philosophy quite lovely. Do you know that song, that one . . . These boys don't know why you come here. They were asking me a few days ago. I told them, it's there in his song. Sing that song.'

Ruhul doesn't know what to do. 'Which song?' he finally asks, 'Whose song? Lalon's?'

'No, baba-ji,' Mijan-maulavi says, 'Hey boy, bring down the dotara. He says he'll sing. No, not the Lalon song about the Prophet. The other one, the one by Photik Gosain, the one about woman-worship. When I was in Rajshahi, in Bangladesh, I heard it from a Meherpur fakir. Oh, what were the words . . . ? Ah yes, I remember a few: "To become a saint, so many take refuge in the feminine." ' Then, after a pause: 'Such lovely words. Such beautiful words. So very true. So, come now, sing. Let the boys listen.'

Ruhul grew grave at this request. How cunning and clever was this man. How far he had thought things through, how well he had laid his plans.

As a boy put the dotara in his hands, someone in his chest let out a howl. 'Why have you come?' he thought, 'Are you seeking sanctuary too? To possess the Prakriti you so desire, what price will you pay today? Are you willing to lose everything? Is your religion so starved?'

Dotara in hand, the fakir leapt to his feet. His body trembled with excitement. His fingers struck the strings and the dotara let out a shriek. Everyone fell silent. Tonu sat still, her eyes aglow.

The fakir began to sing in self-condemnation:

To become a saint, so many take refuge
  in the feminine
On the saint's desire-ocean rise great floods
And the floating market of love passes by

The Kalnagini slithers this way and that across his shoulders. The owl shuts his eyes in pleasure. The golden lizard is sad, and sways slowly from side to side.

Why capture the snake
Without knowing its cure
If the snake bites you
How to keep your soul pure
To become a saint, we worship woman . . .

Ruhul's dotara screams, as though it will split in two, it weeps and wails and howls. The fakir's song, and how helpless he was now, makes Tonu's eyes grow wet with tears. It is as if he has gone mad.

'What were you thinking?' the maulavi snapped as soon as the song stopped, 'Why are you here? Go, boys, you've got your answer. Now let's get on with work. Tell me, fakir, to whom have you come? To the wife of a Muslim man? Hey, Kismat, where are you? We've got to tie him up now, it's time. Lamb's wool and fakir's beard—two such precious things. First feed him beef-roti, a Muslim's favourite food. Then we'll shave him clean. Tonu, my girl, bring him the beef curry. Your husband's sent it earlier. Beef from a barren cow—where is it, where have you kept it?'

'You got the song you wanted,' Ruhul replied firmly, 'Now, no more. I don't eat beef. No beef, no meat, no fish, no egg. I am a vegetarian.'

'Why?'

'Not because the scriptures have denied it. But because we think the body does not need it. It heats the blood, prevents the mind from achieving stillness. Besides, the cow has caused so much hate between Hindus and Muslims—it disgusts me. And that you think you can convert someone with a taste of it—that disgusts me more. The cobblers have spent generations eating off the carcasses of cows, yet they can never become Muslim in your eyes. Back in Swaruppur, my village, I've seen them going from door to door during your festivals, begging for a scrap of meat. But you lot have no pity, you give them nothing. Neither do the Hindus. So the thought of beef saddens me. I stay away from it. The Surah Baqara says—'

'What says?' the maulavi asks at once.

'The Qur'an says. The Surah Baqara says. Baqara means cow. But we interpret it differently. Hindus and Muslims riot over the cow. We say that cows may come in different colours, but their milk is all the same.'

'Yes, cow. But, tell me again, what does the Baqara say? Cows of different colours?'

'Forget your Baqara,' Hajmat exploded, 'If you come to a beef-eating woman, you have to eat beef too—that's my *hadis*, that's our *hadis* and that's Mijan-maulavi's Baqara. Bloody fakir, doesn't know who he's dealing with! Hey, Keramat, sharpen the blade. Shave him clean.'

Mijan-maulavi was a steady man. 'Don't have to get so excited now,' he said, 'Everything will happen, there's enough time. First let me hear what the Baqara says. Come, tell me. Hey, you boy, stir the fire.'

The fire howls back to life.

Meanwhile, Tonu silently latched and locked the door and tucked the keys into the saree folds at her waist.

'In the Surah Baqara,' said Ruhul, 'Allah asked Hazrat Musa to kill a cow. A specific kind of cow. Musa relayed that instruction to the community, told them the cow had to be killed. It was a very strict instruction. This make it obvious that, until then, there had been no ritual of cow slaughter. That's why the instructions had to be given in such detail. There is a history, Miyan-ji.'

'You're right. A strict instruction. That's why if you convert by eating beef, Allah is so pleased. And the cobblers—they eat dead cows, dead meat, not halal meat. Not according to scripture. Not hygienic either. If that meat was good enough, the Baqara wouldn't have been so strict with its instructions. The meat they eat is not qurbani—it has not been ritually sacrificed.'

Ruhul Fakir couldn't help but disagree: 'But isn't a slaughtered cow dead too? The cobblers don't eat half-alive cows. And they don't eat just any dead cow—they make sure they choose the fresh ones. If a fresh cow is all it takes to . . . '

'You bastard!' roared one of the two crisp young men, the one called Keramat, and rushed at Ruhul with an open razor, pushed him to the ground and squatted on his chest. The second one, Kismat, tied his feet tight. Then his hands behind his back. The fakir's words had struck deep into their hearts. Because the cobblers sat on little mats on the floor, banging drums and clanging bells while the pujas took place.

'Good, now the ropes are tied,' said Mijan-maulavi, 'The woman eats, dead or alive. Now the man will eat too. Tonu, my girl, please bring the curry. Feed him with your own loving fingers. We marry girls from other communities to teach them our religion. And this wretched fakir dares seduce our girl into *his* religion! Bring, bring the meat, dear girl.'

'I've thrown it away,' Tonu replies.

Hajmat is furious, the blood rushes to his head. 'I killed the cow as soon as I heard he'd come. And you threw it away!'

He charges at her, still clutching the wooden cattle prod from his ride. Grabs one of her legs as she tries to flee, and beats her again and again. Tonu screams. 'Give me the key,' he roars, 'You've hidden the meat in your room. Give it to me, you bitch. Today's the night of the second talaq. I'll give you the third too if you don't.'

A few moments was all it took to shave the fakir's beard. And then his head. Tonu heard them shouting, saw them carrying the fakir away. Then she blacked out.

After everyone left, Hajmat heaved the inert body of his wife up onto the verandah and raped her.

Then, his mouth against her ear, he said, 'Talaq.'

It was a long time before Tonu regained consciousness. It must have been around midnight. The song of the fakir still hummed in her ears: To become a saint, we take refuge in woman. Tonu's face hardens as she remembers those words. The sky, engraved with a thousand stars. Darkness. Her body, numb with pain. She can't move her legs. The fakir's sad shaven face floats before her. He had wanted sanctuary. Was he still alive? Such a strong person, yet he had cried out in pain. Trembled with fear. His eyes had grown wet with tears. A token resistance was all he'd offered, yet how they had punched and kicked him. Kismat had grabbed his hair and yanked his head this side and that while shearing him. And with every stroke of the blade how the fakir had sobbed.

Finally, they shaved him clean, shaved him bald. His tears had glittered in the firelight. He'd stood there, his head hanging low. Ashamed and humiliated, unable to look up. Silently, the tears had welled up and then rolled down his cheeks.

Kismat yanked his head up. The fakir groaned in pain. His eyes blurred over with tears.

Those eyes met Tonu's.

Hajmat hit her ankle once more. Tonu clenched her teeth, bit back her scream. She knew these men wouldn't listen to reason, they'd beat her to their heart's content, humiliate her absolutely. Hajmat wanted the keys; Tonu said she'd lost them in the dark. Hajmat didn't believe her, he beat her again and again.

The fakir's tear-soaked eyes faded away. Tonu fainted again. The boys had carried him away somewhere. Two tear-soaked humiliated eyes had sought sanctuary but then faded into the dark. 'Never come back, fakir-saheb,' thought Tonu, 'Never come back, not like this, and never speak of cobblers and sweepers. Where will you find the man of gold? All the world is upside down in this darkness, my saint.'

Somehow Tonu gets up and hobbles down to the courtyard. Suddenly, she is startled by a voice: 'Aunt!' It is Rosul, standing near the fence. 'Fakir's lying over there,' he says, 'Across the silt-land. I couldn't untie his knots. Take a chopper with you to cut the ropes.'

Limping heavily, Tonu climbs down onto the silt-land. Stumbling this way and that, she finally finds the fakir. Lying on the V point. His body on this side, his head on that. She draws closer, and then almost flings herself upon him. For a while, neither can speak a word. Then: 'Untie the knots, Tonu,' the fakir says, 'Set me free. They have beaten us like this all along, flung us aside. We have hidden in the darkness, just like this, and found our way again. Come, Tonu, let's go.'

'Where to?' Tonu asks helplessly, 'I can't walk any more.'

Ruhul hoists Tonu onto his shoulders. 'Did you bring my dotara?'

'Yes.'

'The quilt?'

'That must have been taken by Hajmat. Tangled threads of animals and birds.'

Ruhul walks towards the eastern horizon, there where the sun will rise, his clothes streaked wet with the blood from Tonu's ankles. To the left of his chest beats the heart of a *true* Muslim, glows gold the throne of Allah.

The fakir lurches on, on into the east. His Prakriti on his shoulders, his dotara in her hands.

Along the eastern horizon, dawn begins to bloom.

Night Kohl

'The two men who've filed a case to ban the Qur'an—do we know who they are, Mohim? I heard there's going to be an investigation?'

'Don't know,' Mohim replied tersely.

'Who are these people fighting for the sharia? Are they local Muslims or have they come from outside?'

'Don't know.'

'This morning, I saw two bald saffron-clad monks on the street. Did you see them too? Where are they from?'

'Don't know that either.'

'They were in a shiny taxi, scattering handbills and books, making grumbling noises through the microphone stuck to the roof of the car. Did you hear them?'

'No. I told you.' Mohim was quite irritated now.

'Two new posters on our wall this morning. Are they yours?'

'No, not at all. We haven't . . . or maybe we have. What do they say?'

'I didn't memorize them.'

'Do you ever memorize our posters, Pishi?' Mohim said and couldn't help burst out laughing.

'Yes, sometimes,' said Sharada-pishi, 'Spelling errors on posters and signboards—they look so bad. Your lot spelt "current" as "currant" the other day. It took me a long time to figure it out. "Evolution" had become "revolution". What all they write! Sometimes they give me headaches, those posters. The same goes for "gunns". Does the extra *n* show that you lot are better armed? You and your friends are the higher-ups—but you don't write those slogans. You'll lose respect if you do. They write, the lower-down ignoramuses. Perhaps most of them learn their alphabets by writing on walls—no?'

Mohim's face grew dark at her words. Then, trying to change the topic, he said, 'Do you want to go to Tarakeshwar? At Shib–Kalitola, they're selling those bamboo poles, the ones for the water pots. Decorated with plastic flowers, bells. Shall I get one for you? Smear some sandalwood paste on your forehead, shout "Bholey-baba paar karega" and set off with the next group of pilgrims. One lot is leaving, Mukul was saying, from Radha Ghat. Do you want to go?'

Mohim, about to put some food in his mouth, looked up at his hand-fan-waving, fly-shooing pishi (a powercut had brought the overhead fan to a halt). Pishi's face had grown hard with pain. She said nothing, but her lips seemed to quiver with some stifled emotion. The fan in her hand stopped waving. The corners of her eyes slowly began to glisten with tears.

'Are you joking with me, Mohim?' Pishi finally asked, her voice low and deep. 'Did I ever say I wanted to go to Tarakeshwar? Why do you lose your temper whenever someone finds fault with you?'

Ashamed, Mohim brought his hand down to his plate. 'No, no, Pishi. It's not that. I'm not joking. You're getting angry for no reason. You really did want to go to Tarakeswar—didn't you?'

'Yes, I did. But with a flowers-and-bells-strung bamboo on my shoulder—why did you think that? Why I wanted to go—you are a communist, so you haven't understood. The communists of this land have never understood this land at all! So how will you understand me, Mohim!'

Pishi dropped her fan to the floor and got to her feet. Then slowly walked out of the kitchen. Suddenly Mohim felt in his heart a peculiar ache. Pishi was not a widow—but her husband was lost, no doubt. Only two years into their marriage and he'd suddenly disappeared. So many pilgrimage sites, so many temple grounds— they'd searched everywhere . . . Every now and then, they'd hear a rumour that he'd become a sannyasi. But whenever they reached his address, he was gone. Yes, he'd been there—but then left, two days ago, for somewhere else. Then, another rumour. Then Baba and Sharada-pishi would set off again. Then return again, with nothing but disappointment. A strange existence, as puzzling as a riddle. Pishi had once been keen to visit Tarakeshwar, buoyed by a sliver of hope that her husband may be there. Then one day she decided that no, she wouldn't go. Hence, the pretty bamboo poles, the painted water pots and the tinkling bells—they no longer bore any relation to Pishi's searching soul. Had no place in her seeker's life. So, shame! Shame on him for bringing it up! Mohim grew sadder and sadder as he thought of Pishi's fate. He couldn't eat any more. He washed up and went to his room. Dried his hands on a towel, put a few mouri grains in his mouth and lit a cigarette. Walked over to the window and looked out at Pishi's tulsi plant.

The tulsi was withering away. Mohim was a History (Hons) student. To him, now, the tulsi plant appeared as a powerful, almost infallible, symbol. 'How will you understand me, Mohim!' Those words flapping their wings like a bird inside his chest. Beating their heads and crying like doves . . . The plant was dying. Mohim could see clearly the dullness of its leaves, their wilting shyness. Pishi had been requesting him almost every day to ask Akul Sardar to get some soil for it. Pishi would give the plant no other. It had been brought from the Ghorapir mazar in Madhurkul. The tulsi is a sensitive plant.

Won't take to any soil but its own. This own-soil–other-soil—this backward mentality Mohim thought repellent. So he hadn't bothered to get in touch with Akul. Turned a deaf ear to Pishi's requests.

Pishi believed that soil had other virtues too. His father suffered from constipation. Pishi said if she fed him rice cooked on an oven made out of that soil, it would cure him. So: 'Tell Akul to bring a little extra.'

'Why Akul?' Mohim had snapped at her yesterday. 'Akul is a thief! How will his stolen soil help your plant or Baba's constipation? Such senseless superstitions! How you passed the Matric, and to what end, I really can't tell! Some holy man somewhere, some thief from somewhere else—what you get by believing all this I just don't understand!'

Pishi had been hurt yesterday too. 'How will you understand the glory of the earth, Mohim?' she'd said, 'You people will need a lot more time to do so.'

What she said yesterday and what she said today—the words were in the same vein. They sprang from the same truth. It was growing clearer to Mohim, growing more puzzling too.

'Yes, Akul is a thief,' Pishi had said, 'But a thief of our times. That's why he still has some *standards*. He has some things that you don't.'

Mohin had been furious. 'Even if a thief has nectar, it would be stolen nectar. I find it strange that you can defend a thief!'

The blow had been a hard one. Pishi had been silent for a while. Then, smiling faintly, she'd said, 'Yes, my son, I find it strange too. Such a wonderful, dream-divined thing—how could he have got it?'

'Dream-divined?' Mohim had stared at Pishi.

'Yes, a dream dispensation, a gift. Akul's father, on his deathbed, gave it to his son. It's name is Night Kohl. Pilu's mother had night-blindness. Akul gave her that kohl to apply for a week. Now she sees everything clearly. Yes, it belongs to a thief. Yet the magic that lies in the heart of it—that no reason can explain. Life does not only follow the path of reason, Mohim. It has other forms of grace too. That story of the night kohl is wonderful indeed.'

At the sight of Pishi's face beginning to glow with joy, Mohim had grown more and more irate. 'Leave it, Pishi,' he'd snapped, 'I don't want to hear that story. What you've drowned your life in—I feel so ashamed when I think about it. Yes, ashamed. And sad. I feel like bursting into tears. Such darkness! What are we doing to prevent it? Alas, nothing is helping!'

Then, with a muffled cry of despair, Mohim had run out of the house. He'd been so agitated that he could barely breathe. But this anguish, this sense of failure, this sense of achieving nothing, none of this was personal. Beneath this agitation, another very real battle was coursing through his veins. The case against the Qur'an in court; the malice of the saffron-clad monks' at their discovery of cow slaughter in the Surah Baqara; the recent clamour about the sharia; the use of cow and pig fat in soaps and detergents; the trident painted on wall after wall—all these made his subconscious bleed.

But what truly terrified him was another reality, the looming threat of riots. Daluidanga, Kakurgachi, Bajitpur, Methidanga, Naskarpur—each place was seething. Twenty years ago, there had been riots in these same villages. He'd heard about them from Pishi. He'd never seen a riot himself, so he didn't not know how that terrible fire began, nor how it extinguished all life. Nor did he know how to stamp out its flames.

If there is a riot now, what will Mohim, his party and his politics do? What will happen? In these questions lie the seeds of his agitation. Before Mohim's eyes, Pishi suddenly assumed the form of an adversary. In truth, while arguing with Pishi, Mohim had come to feel more and more helpless. As though he were a poisonous snake lunging at thin air, that all the poison of life had cascaded up his throat. As though the essence of sin had crawled out of the deepest cave and was now setting him on fire . . . Mohim felt very alone.

The riots had broken out twenty years ago, the accounts of which Pishi knew by heart. The riots of those days were far less complicated. In those days, you could tell the bloodthirsty ones by their dhotis and beards, their lungis and tiki-poiteys. These days, no such signs were needed. Or, the signs had changed. A thick moustache, a cross hanging round a neck, a kada round a wrist—neither Hindu nor Muslim.

These thoughts send a shudder through Mohim. The thought that, twenty years ago, there'd been no case against the Qur'an, no fat mixed with soap, no discovery of cow slaughter in the Surah Baqara, no determination to argue for the sharia. And yet . . . Pishi had finally found a natural explanation: 'Eid and Dol fell on the same day,' she'd suddenly said, 'The seasons are different in Arabia and Bengal. But in time, somehow, Dol and Eid came together, fell on the same moon. That was it.'

'But both are happy festivals,' Mohim said, '*Coloured festivals.*'

'So? Shashanka's son Netai, his pichkiri splashed old Muslim Mobarak's new attar-scented Eid kurta. That was it. That was the real reason. Understand, Mohim? But why God brought Eid and Dol together—no one had religiosity enough to fathom that. Man's faith is good. But his fervour is not. Sense and reason are not the same. Sense holds within it compassion while reason swells with the arrogance of logic. Yes, my son. That compassion—our father called it the supreme compassion—is lost from life.'

Mohim wanted to know the real reason behind the riots. He was not interested in the differences between faith and fervour, nor did he feel any enthusiasm for any supreme compassion. He was, rather, desirous of the beauty of reason. Riots could never be natural, he believed. That logic could comfort Pishi but Mohim could not subscribe to it. Isn't that so?

The sun set slowly in the western sky. Darkness began to fall. The pallor of the tulsi seemed to have intensified. Beside it, the sandhyamoni flowers bloomed in a sad profusion. These were Pishi's flowers, sorrowing and soft. Yet. Thoughts of supreme compassion, of the night kohl, of the secret of the mazar's soil—how they played in Pishi's mind, what their tricks and mysteries were, Mohim could never fathom. Why not? Suddenly Mohim felt as though he didn't know Pishi at all. The Pishi who, providing a natural explanation for a riot, effortlessly moved on to supreme compassion, who was nostalgic for a time when even thieves had a *standard*, whose sense of medicine lay in curing constipation with rice cooked on a clay oven . . . Who was Pishi really?

Twilight was fast disappearing. Was it preparing for the riots? Darkness thickened, slowly, gradually. This earth was so old. The edge of the sky, as still as the time of ancient man. The moon was pushing its way up in the east, bit by bit. Like a *magic* trick. Mohim sat on the *rok* and watched it rise.

Pishi was sprinkling water on her tulsi. Seeing her face, you could tell she wasn't angry any more. 'I'm water-witching this tulsi,' she said. 'The tulsi doesn't live on water, after all. It lives in the earth. But—Akul hasn't come yet.'

Pishi sighed. Lit the oil lamp. Wrapped the end of her saree round her shoulders and bowed low. By the glow of the lamp, she looked more tender, more pure. 'Every day,' she whispered, 'at this time, I feel the pain of separation. I can tell you without shame, son, that it hurts. I have only one puja . . . But today, Mohim, the azan has not happened. It seems there is no avoiding the riots. We did not hear the imam today. Look at the Roza moon, Mohim—see how black it's become.'

Mohim's heart was hammered by twin blows—the black moon, the riots! Pishi's only puja!

How astonishing! Pishi had no other puja! The thought ran through him like a jolt of electricity. Pishi said such strange things. She'd noticed there'd been no azan that evening.

'How will you know me, Mohim?' asks that figure drenched in love's loss, 'You're a communist.'

Mohim gets up and goes to his room, overcome with melancholy. Pishi was lighting incense sticks near the tulsi. Soon she'd come into the house, walk with them from room to room, wafting scented smoke, then go into her own room and place them at the foot of her Saraswati-picture calendar.

Pishi's shadow on the veranda, the shadow of the smoke on the wall. As if Pishi's shadow had caught fire, was billowing smoke. Was Pishi burning? Then how is she so happy, so full of smiles?

Pishi came into Mohim's room. 'Every evening, when I listen to Imam Ali's azan, I remember a story. That pain of separation I mentioned—this story is about that. You never want to listen to any of my stories. But we had some brave moments in our lives too. Yes, we did.'

Mohim sat up in amazement. Story! Bravery! What was she saying? Such words from a tulsi devotee seemed to engulf him in puzzlement.

'Sharada? Are you home, Sharada?'

An unfamiliar voice. At this hour, whose soft and serene voice was that, calling out Pishi's name? Mohim and Pishi grew wary. After a few moments, the call came again. A bit of light from the first-floor window fell upon the courtyard. Someone came in and stood in that faint light.

(The first floor was inhabited by Mohim's father, the bedridden Pulin Mukherjee. Mohim rarely went up to meet him. Pishi was Pulin's primary caregiver. There was also another woman, a nurse. She often lent a hand with some of the household chores. This first floor casts very little shadow upon our story. Which is why, to this call, there was no response from that floor.)

Mohim has no mother. Pishi was the one who'd kept him in the shade of maternal love. Surely she was his friend too.

Mohim came out into the courtyard. Pishi came out too. 'I've come to see you, Sharada,' the visitor said, 'But I'd like to have a few words with Mohim too.'

Sharada recognized Imam Ali.

'Imam-bhai, you! I can't believe it. See, how even in the dark I've recognized you! Come, come in. Don't stay standing in the courtyard. Just a while ago I was telling Mohim about you.'

Imam Ali walked into the room full of light. 'About me? Me?' Imam Ali was astonished. 'Why? I'm a simple khatib. A poor Muslim. You are Charulata's sister. A rich man's daughter, a Brahman. Why would you talk about me?'

Mohim noticed that Pishi was embarrassed and changed the subject, 'No . . . not about you, really. About your azan. You didn't read the azan today.'

'Yes, I did. Only, you didn't hear it.'

'You did? When?'

'I did. As I do every day, at the same time and in the same place. But I didn't use the loudspeaker. That's why you didn't hear it. A policeman came and turned off the mike. From tomorrow, you won't be able to hear the Sehri at dawn either. That's why I've come to Mohim—if he can do something. See, it's because I read the azan that you still talk of me. That's no bad thing.'

'Yes, Khatib-saheb,' Mohim said, finding a crack in the conversation that let him speak, 'we were talking about your azan and had almost started talking about you when you arrived.'

'No, Mohim,' Pishi said, 'Not him. I was about to tell you a different story . . . I'd suddenly remembered Chhordi, my sister.'

Mohim noticed that Pishi's face was flushed. 'I knew a story was coming,' he said, smiling, 'But I didn't know it was going to be Charu-pishi's story. This is the first I'm hearing of her!'

'You and your habit of joking about everything,' Pishi chided him gently, 'Why don't you ask Imam-bhai about Akul and the night kohl? How amazing it is! Imam-bhai, remember?'

Imam Ali was sitting on the sofa. With his grey-flecked hair and beard, he was such a dignified presence. A slight smile played on his lips. His eyes, large and beautiful, sparkled. The air was fragrant with incense and Pishi's tobacco. On Imam Ali's broad forehead glowed the dust-mark of the sijda. A long kurta, a lungi. A watch on his right wrist. An old Parker pen clipped to his breast pocket.

Mohim and Pishi were sitting, side by side, on the bed.

At Pishi's question, the smile on Imam Ali's face grew broader. 'This evening, Sharada, when I sat to pray, I was close to tears. My heart was wracked with despair. Why only Akul—there were so many more whom I was remembering. Could we imagine in our wildest dreams that the azan would be stopped? We Muslims are so few in these parts. Across all these villages, this is the only big mosque. If even that mosque is not allowed its azan, can you imagine just where the blow falls, Mohim?'

'Even I could not believe my ears at first, Khatib-saheb,' Mohim said, 'Nor could my party. We're all stunned by the thana's behaviour. We're all feeling like fools. This is very wrong. I promise you, our party will say as much as it can, do as much as possible. We will go to the police station. Take a *deputation*. Exactly which Hindus are behind this—we're looking into it, all right?'

'Apparently the azan disturbs the Hindus' sleep. Because we use the mike at Sehri time to call out to roza-keepers, some Hindus are angry. Yet, in my childhood, in Madhurkul, I've seen . . .' He fell silent for a few moments. Then: 'I've seen Jyathamoshai, Sharada's father, listen to the azan with such concentration. If the children made a ruckus, he'd get angry and scold them. "Don't make a noise now," Jethima, his wife, would warn them, keep them quiet: "Your father's listening to the azan." I've seen all this. Remember, Sharada? We Muslims would ask him why he listened to the azan like that. He would not really answer—just smile and say, "It's very nice, very nice. When I hear the tune, my mind floats off to some other place. Tunes have no caste or creed, after all. I listen to the tunes, and I know that the words are in praise of the lord. Can the azan rob me of my caste?" '

'Wait, Imam-bhai,' said Pishi, suddenly emotional. She had finally found a kindred spirit for her nostalgia. Unlocked the innumerable doors of memory. Oppressed, outraged and disturbed by their present, they were—Mohim felt—being propelled back into their past.

'Every year, in front of our Chandi temple,' Pishi said, 'Baba would organize a Muharram feast for all of you. Every year, a group of you would come and show off your stick-fighting skills. Our maternal cousin Srikanto was a brilliant dhol-player. Such a dhol-durbar there'd be! Such a booming it set off in the heart. How the Muharram taziyeh would sparkle, how grand would be the processions! Baba would spring up, grab a stick from one of you, whirl it in the air a few times and say, "Imam Ali'll play now. Lay your bets, Shamsuddi." A stick-fight in a temple courtyard—it's the stuff of stories now! Impossible to believe in this day and age.'

Pishi drew a breath, then carried on: 'Imam's stick-fighting skills were legendary. When he stood up to play, everyone froze in excitement. And how he wielded that stick—as though cracking thunderbolts in the air. We'd watch, hypnotized! And my sister—her heart seemed to feel every blow. Of course, Imam-bhai did not know that. No one but I did. There's no harm in saying all this now—that's why I'm saying it. Does it embarrass you, Imam-bhai?'

Imam looked down at the floor. 'In those days,' he said slowly, 'Hindus like your father had assumed the responsibility of protecting the Muslim minorities. This area always had fewer Muslims. Under those circumstances, the courage of a Hindu girl could not be shared by a Muslim boy. The Hindus always had greater mental strength . . . For his time, Jyathamoshai was a different kind of man altogether.'

'We last met you,' Pishi said, 'near the Shiva temple, under the banyan tree. Chhordi and I had gone there, with pots full of milk, to pour on the sign of Shiva. The family was talking of getting Chhordi married. Those days, girls were married off quite early. On our way back, we met you. But at first we couldn't tell it was you. You'd grown such a long and thick beard! Your new appearance startled Chhordi. "Imam," she said, "why have you become so much of a Muslim?" Such terrible words, no? Chhordi had been in great pain for a while. "Charulata," you'd told her, "you have become so much of a Hindu." I remember. Simple words to say and hear, but in those days they meant much more. In those days, Muslim boys would suddenly grow beards and wear long kurtas and caps and become "properly" Muslim. The Hindus didn't mind—in fact, they'd be quite pleased. Nor did the Muslims mind if Hindu boys became more properly Hindu. It was all only natural. But, even today, I think about why Chhordi disapproved of your becoming so much of a Muslim . . . even today I think about what her words truly meant.'

Pishi's story held Mohim almost in thrall. Really, he had never truly known her. Now he felt almost afraid of what greater enchantment she was leading him towards. Almost as if she was revealing to him a vast mysterious and entirely unknown world of wonder, room by innermost room.

'Even today,' Mohim finally said, 'a Muslim boy can suddenly set everything aside and grow a beard, don a cap. It has happened in our party too. Red-flag waving Sirajul, slogan-shouting Sirajul—suddenly he walked into the mosque and became a khatib. A shameful truth—I confess it now. We could not save Sirajul. He is still with the party but he has become Muslim.'

'But this becoming,' Pishi said, 'this you will understand, Imambhai. Becoming then, and becoming now—they are not the same. They are entirely different. Sirajul and Imam are different people. I'm only saying what I've understood.'

'The people are different, true,' Mohim said, 'but what happened is the same. They both found religion, both rediscovered faith. What the attraction is, I wonder.'

'It's a feeling within, Mohim. A very natural feeling. What happened to Imam stemmed from an inner maya. We all have that magic in us—we are replete with it. I think Sirajul had suffered some blow. So he ran away from your hounding. What have you given to the people that they will stay with you? One kilo of wheat? One licence? Police protection? Then what about the three Hindu policemen who came and turned off the mike? Can a man's heart be set afire only by the colour of your flag? A man needs food for his soul too, needs courage, needs fulfilment. Which of these have you given?'

An agitated Pishi got off the bed and left the room. Then returned a few minutes later, sprinkling incense powder on a clay fireholder and blowing at the sparks, trying to make the fire catch. The room soon grew hazy with fragrant smoke, its coils as though clustering around and clutching at Pishi.

'So we have given nothing to the people?' Mohim asked. 'Done nothing?'

'Yes, you have. Of course you have,' Pishi wanted to respond. Instead, she said: 'You have hounded that maya away. Hounded by reason, that maya now hides in some deep dark corner of life. But it lives still—you have not been able to kill it. It lives, it lives. That maya, that magic—they transform Ratnakar into Valmiki. I have seen Paran. Seen Akul. Seen the thief's kohl. The spells and enchantments cast by witches and crones. The kohl that ended up changing Paran's life. Made him stop being a thief. Made him tell his son, "Don't ever sell this night kohl to another thief. Give it to honest people, help them cure their eyes." So, how does a man change from thief to saint? Through maya, through magic. Just as Nasuha the Robber changed. His story is in the *hadis*-Qur'an. Imam-bhai will know it well. Paran told my father he'd put the night kohl in his eyes and set off to steal. Even on a moonless night, the kohl let him see things as clear as day . . . But that maya—that maya remains no more.'

'We read the khutbah on Fridays,' Imam said, 'It has a section, the Taubatun Nasuha. Nasuha the robber, the one who stole shrouds from graves and sold them, the one who had sex with female corpses in their graves, who raped them, that robber Nasuha was moved to tauba, to great repentance. He remains a great example of how totally one may repent and weep for one's sins.'

'What do the criminals do now?' said Pishi, 'They commit bigger crimes. Nobody becomes Paran. Nobody becomes Nasuha. Why not? The one's who'll start the riot—who are they? Who will put the night kohl in their eyes? Crooks, every one. The Muslims have no one. The Hindus have no one either. But what saddens me is something else. Shall I tell you what it is, Imam-bhai?'

Imam nodded, eagerly.

Mohim looked at Pishi, his eyes blurred with incense smoke.

'When we were young,' Pishi said, 'you and Chhordi and I went so often to Ghorapir's mazar. Listened to the powerful pir reciting the azan from his grave. There was a tulsi there, planted on a pedestal, people lit oil lamps round its base. We'd eat the batashas that the devout offered in prayer. When we put our ears to the tulsi pedestal, we could hear the pir's azan. Really, if we listened very carefully, we could hear his voice. When I got married, Akul got me a sapling from that plant. When I place my ears against its pedestal, I can hear the azan too. When I lost my husband, I came away to Mohim's house and brought the tulsi with me.'

'Can you still hear the azan, Sharada?' Imam asked. Pishi said nothing. Then, after a few moments, she said: 'No. Not any more. I used to. But not any more. Slowly, ever so slowly, it has stopped. But what force has throttled that sound—that I do not know. Have I become too much of a Hindu? I should be more at peace then, shouldn't I? But then why am I in such pain? Have I lost the last bit of that maya? Or is it something else? Why do I feel so much pain, Mohim—why don't you tell me?'

'Can something be done for us, Mohim?' asked Imam.

The girl who helped Pishi about the house walked in with tea and biscuits.

'It can,' Mohim said, 'Now please have some tea. Go back to the mosque. Don't worry. Rest assured.'

'How can I rest, Mohim? They are spreading vile rumours about me, that I'm an agent of Saudi Arabia. That I'm a spy. That I've taken photos of our mosque and sent it to the Saudi government, asking for money for renovations. That I've taken bribes from Pakistan. Tell me, Sharada, can any of this be true? Though not all the Hindus believe in this propaganda, some of them are regarding me with suspicion. Thinking: Maybe it's true, who knows how people really are. So how can I not worry? My heart is shrinking, son.'

Pishi picked up a cup of tea from the tray and placed it before Imam. 'Drink,' she said softly.

Talks began at the party office. 'We need to enquire into every detail,' Sudipto said, 'and find out what happened and why. Who went to the police and convinced the OC to stop the mike? What was their logic? And the OC—why did he rush over to the mosque? Under the circumstances, what role are the Muslims themselves playing? We must examine every aspect before coming to a decision. If necessary, we'll have to go and talk to the police. If necessary, we'll have to conduct discussions in every neighbourhood, every locality, and try and restore a healthy atmosphere.'

'No healthy atmosphere can be restored, comrade,' said Imran, slightly heatedly, 'Debates and discussions, processions and hand-bills—these will not help us cope with this situation. From the Maghrib to the Isha and the Tahajjud, right up to midnight, Imam's mosque is packed with people. We've never seen such huge turnouts for the namaz before. It's quite alarming. And this has hurt all their sentiments. We had no clue about it either—we were caught off-guard. I'm frightened—going home late feels full of *risk*. I'm unable to make the Muslims understand. The Hindus are holding secret meetings. Apparently they're going to call some famous religious leader to speak. In response, the Muslims are planning a huge majlis. Why are you taking this situation so lightly?'

'I'm not taking it lightly at all, Imran-sahib,' Sudipto said. 'Why don't you tell us what your *suggestions* are?'

'My suggestion would be to change the OC. Replace Lalit-babu with Sultan Khan. For some time, there has been talk of this happening. Sultan Khan has fantastic *tackling* skills. He is tough and fearless. If he comes, the police will not become impartial but at least the situation will acquire some kind of balance. Right now, all three officers at the police station are Hindu. If Sultan Khan comes, the Muslims will feel reassured.'

'Will you feel reassured too?' Sudipto asked.

Imran tugged at the edge of his collar and said in a wounded voice, 'Yes, of course.'

'How will you feel reassured? As a Muslim or as an Indian?'

'I . . . see,' mumbled a slightly stumped Imran.

'No, you don't see,' Sudipto said in tones of mild reproach, 'Sultan Khan's strength, his lack of fear, his competence—all this because he's a Muslim or because he's a policeman? How are we supposed to judge him?'

'But,' said Imran, his face glum, 'you're not understanding the situation.'

'Suddenly,' Mohim interrupted, 'if Sultan Khan arrives in the middle of these complicated and critical times, I think it more likely that the riots *will* occur. Besides, our principles are more important. So what if all three officers are Hindu? We only want that the police remain impartial. If the Muslims see that we have convinced the Hindu officers to protect their life and limb, to protect their religious rights, will not that be better, Imran-bhai?'

'Your words are always comforting, Mohim-bhai. But such words do not save lives. Tell me, have we succeeded in becoming communists? All we seem to do is go from one election to the next. Am I a Hindu or a communist or a Muslim? I wonder when this dilemma will be resolved. Goodbye, comrade.' And with a red salaam, Imran left the party office and disappeared into the milling crowds on the street.

The next day, posters covered every wall: 'Sultan Khan, go away! Sultan Khan, go back!' Then another one: 'Down with Lalit-Officer.' Then, yet another: 'Three Hindu officers in one police station! State Government, tell us why.' And: 'Bring back the mike in our mosque.'

Mohim read the posters and his whole being felt wracked with pain. He was on the way to the party office but stopped mid-way the moment he realized that all the posters were from his party. And that the orders must have come from the very top. As he read them, he saw in his party's words their deadly opportunism. They please the Hindus, the please the Muslims too. Elections come, elections go. Life stays the same.

Dusk falls. Suddenly a young man runs past, panting, running for his life. Followed by three men, sickles gleaming in their hands, speeding down the lane like arrows. Brushing past Mohim. Mohim cannot tell if they are Hindu or Muslim.

Mohim rushes home.

The next day, he heard that Imam Ali had been beheaded inside the mosque. And in Jugipara, the headless body of Hindu Haradhan, Nagen's young son, had been found beside his father's loom.

Mohim stays in his room all day. Doesn't say a word. Pishi is shocked at his appearance—Mohim seems to have become an old man overnight.

Pishi's tulsi withers some more . . . Evening falls. The sandhya-moni blooms. The incense glows. Mohim looks at Pishi. When will she worship the tulsi? Evening was almost over. Was Pishi waiting for something? Won't Pishi light the lamp? What has happened to Pishi today?

'Pishi, won't you water the tulsi today?'

'I will, son.'

'When, Pishi? Evening's almost over. Where is your lamp? Does it have enough oil?'

'It does, son.'

'When will you light it?'

'Let the azan be over. Then.'

'There won't be any azan today, Pishi.'

Mohim's voice is choked. Pishi, striking a match, says, 'The patterns of life are so strange, Mohim. The azan will start and I'll light the lamp—that's one pattern. But that pattern seems to be unravelling. In my heart, the azan will echo always. In my heart, it will always ask for light.'

Pishi's lamp begins to glow. By that light, Mohim thinks that Pishi looks different somehow. As if she is not Sharada but Charulata. The Charulata who was still waiting for the azan, who had not been able to bow low in prayer.

Mohim sees this maya-magical moment slowly melt into the darkness. Dissolve into the night. There is no light to be seen. The moon is covered by a patch of a terrible black cloud. It doesn't move an inch. In the sky stands still the sky of the ancient clans.

Mohim's heart is empty. He is entirely alone. As though he is nightblind.

The Road

The gravel road, red at the mouth, on its way through Goyash and Kalikapur villages and running on, beyond the Harirampur ghat towards Lalbagh, tore through Khodadil's courtyard and split it in two. The bedrooms were divided and now fell one on each side; not only that, the kitchen now lay in the south and the stable in the north. Even more absurd: Khodadil noticed incredulously that his horse was stamping its hooves in the north while its cart lay in the south. To attach the cart to the horse, the horse had to be pulled from north to south by its harness, all the while keeping an eye on the road and the passing jumble of men and cycles and bullock carts. That life was one big folly, about that there was no doubt.

Some people referred to Khodadil—Allah-in-his-heart—as Ghoradil—horse-in-his-heart. Not that this displeased him entirely. Once in a while he thought to himself that the nickname perhaps disrespected the Lord more than it did him. He was, in truth, Dilu Tanga-wala—Dilu, the carriage driver. It was on the back of this horse that Imam Husayn had fought the Battle of Karbala, a colossal and magnificent encounter. In that clash of thirst and blood, the mane of the horse had been drenched with dew from the sky, its belly grown sweaty in the passion of the battle, its breath panted laments for Asgar, mourning like a Jarigan:

Snake at right, jackal at left
Move your feet slow, step by step
O don't let Asgar go to war—
O mother Sahrban
The horse is trembling
O don't let Asgar go to war—

Dilu too had his own battle, his battle of life. Every day he had to go to war. His household depended on the sweat and blood of this horse that pulled his cart. Whether there be snake to the right or unlucky jackal to the left, he had no choice but to ferry passengers to town. The road's red rubble turned to dust under the cartwheels; the horse's tail grew coated with red dust; with red mud in the monsoons; with red dew in the winter. Yet the majestic Dulduli's bells jingled on.

Dilu's problem was that there was no one he had to confide in. That this red road had split him into two, like a piece of cloth—to whom to complain? In any case, he truly was a horse-hearted man, the road was his life. The road was why he had the horse, why he existed at all. The road had been a dirt road before; then it was laid over with gravel, became crackling-crisp red. On the old road, after the rains, when the slush dried up and it grew navigable again, rickshaws had carried people to and from town. The gravel destroyed the road; bits of brick and gaping craters reduced it to a long stretch of bumps and potholes.

The Bhoirab river, flowing alongside, flooded half the road during the monsoon. The silt of the saline flood-waters ate away the jaw and palate of the road, corroded its body. The road would then become dangerous for the rickshaws. Even when the waters ebbed, the bumpy red surface would refuse to smoothen out. The rickshaws gave up, but the leper-cheeked, broken-jawed, half-gnawed-at palate of the road could not defeat his Dulduli, his Tiger. Swerving, slithering, starting and sliding, twisting and turning—he carried his passengers to and fro. Last year, he had even managed to drag back from town Gopal Haji's fat wife, even though the bumpy ride had badly scraped the poor woman's ample waist. The wheels had almost come off, but held; the woman's bones, though, had been thoroughly shaken.

A click of the tongue and a swish of the whip were the keys to steer the majestic Dulduli. If the road was blackened over with tar, as Dilu had heard it might be, rendered smooth like the surface of a palm, then the rickshaws would flock back in hundreds. The road then would swallow him whole like a python, him and horse and cart, all of them. Let not red become black pitch, O Lord. O woe Rasul, what kind of thought was this!

'What are you thinking, headman's-son?'

'The road.'

'The road's not gone anywhere, my father-in-law's son. There it is, running straight ahead. Sometimes I feel it'll rush right into the womb, startle the babes asleep in the dark. You have to cross this road to come to your woman at night, in the dark. Doesn't it make your heart ache? Don't you feel ashamed? Aren't you a comrade? Can't you bend the road? Can't you twist its tail? Do it—let me see how much of a man you are! Can you?'

'No, Sunabhan. No, my wife, I can't.' From deep in his throat, a sigh rolls out. And Khodadil stares silently at his horse.

Dilu knew that his children were asleep in one of the road-split rooms. He knew how sweet was the nectar of sleep, the honey of slumber. Yet the poor things kept starting awake—all night long, crowds walked back from the market, brokers and touts, cyclists went to and fro. Some nights, it was herds of cows being smuggled into Bangladesh. All night long, this red road rattled and rolled. The children kept jerking awake. And their disturbed sleep had shredded to bits his conjugal life. This road seemed to lick the heart of man's sex with its tongue. As if, truly, it wanted to enter his woman's womb.

Yet, once, the road had lain so gently and peacefully beside his house. A government-survey report is what let it stride into his home and rend it asunder. Khodadil could do nothing. No carriage driver could stake a claim once the Public Works Department had issued a decree. Nor make a complaint at the panchayat. The leader had said: The road is progress. If we don't give people progress, they won't want us any more. Dilu-bhai, don't worry. You'll get compensation. Your horse needs a road, too, isn't that so?'

'How long will the road stay red, Shiben-da?'

'Tar's been spread and roller-smoothened as far as the edge of Kalikapur market. It'll grow black very soon, not stay red for much longer. When the city enters the village, it turns the dirt road red. Then black. Such are the rules of progress. What's the colour of your horse, Dilu-bhai?'

'Pitch black, Shiben-da.'

'Then what are you worried about? A black horse is the symbol of progress—remember that, and don't lose heart.'

'You're not making fun of me, are you?'

'No. We are telling everyone about how you are suffering in silence.'

'I'm an orphan. This black horse is my father, my mother. So what if its black? I'm black too. So will the road be. And soon will be everything else. Good, the way progress is coming. One day my wife had put mehndi on the white patch on my horse's forehead. Turned it red. You'd liked it, remember?'

'I do indeed. You'll get your compensation, Dilu.'

'How much?'

'Let's see.'

Fifteen hundred rupees was fixed as compensation. But, at the last moment, Khodadil changed his mind. And astonished them all by saying, 'I'd like to donate it to progress, Shiben-da. I'd like to donate my courtyard. Write it down and let everyone know.' And with that he strode out of the party office. Though newly lettered, Dilu refused to sign his name and claim that sum of money.

Leaving the office, Dilu walked along the road for a bit, all the way to the tea stall beneath the pakurh tree at Motilaltala. There, his horse was grazing by the side of the high road, the cart waiting in the shade of the tree. He sat down on a bamboo bench. Sat in silence for a while, then ordered a glass of tea and a bun. After his snack, he lit a purple-string-tied bidi with his lighter.

Smoke engulfed his moustache and rose up into the air. Dilu wiped his face and neck with the gamchha hanging round his shoulders. How hot it was, the sweat was trickling down his legs, all the way down to his bone-crushing sandals. The black-thread-strung talisman tied round his neck glittered in the sun.

Passengers don't like a cart with a rickety horse. If you don't feed your horse well, how will it grow strong? Rice-bran powder, oilcakes, starch, corn husk, grass, molasses, chapattis and gram. Green peas and green pulses to make its skin shine, like lightning. Khodadil had a loofah, and special scissors too. The mane needed grooming. And the eyes always needed to be clean. You needed to treat it like a guest. Address it with reverence. Only then to one snap of your finger, or a click of your tongue, the horse-tiger will fly, as if on wings.

If not? It will fall asleep while trotting. It will stop when the wheel is stuck in a ditch. Shake its head helplessly. Then no matter how hard you whip it, it won't move an inch—it will just stand there and bleat. This creature is the Qased of Karbala, the messenger of war. That's why they say, 'from the horse's mouth.'

A horse brings us news of blood and thirst and sweat. News of where the traveller has strayed. News of where a hero lies dead in a ditch. What news is there that dear Dulduli will not bring home to us? The black horse of the red road, the fierce tiger. The froth of life bubbling at its mouth. Sometimes Dilu called him 'sweetie'; sometimes, 'tiger'. He couldn't pronounce sweetie—his Murshidabadi tongue made it 'swootie'.

Returning the empty glass and paying for the tea and bun with money from his full-shirt pocket, Dilu walked over to his horse. He made sure Sweetie was always well groomed. A red ribbon round his fore- head; a gold-plated silver medal round his neck; plastic flowers tied to the ribbon, gleaming like fire; small bells stitched to the belt round his neck. Sometimes Dilu made him marigold garlands. His tail was always beautifully combed. His whole body gleamed, polished with the oil of grace.

'Swootie,' Dilu called, his voice full of love.

Tiger was nibbling the sparse grass by the roadside. He looked up at his master's voice. Sniffed at Dilu once, then bent his neck to affectionately nuzzle his master's shoulder. As if he was whispering advice to Dilu.

'I didn't take that money, Tiger. I donated my courtyard to the government. Didn't I do right?'

Tiger seemed to nod in approval.

'Now people will watch the pride of the horse-cart driver.'

'Chihihichihihi,' Tiger said.

'But what Sunabhan will say—that's what I'm worried about, my dear.'

'Hrrrsohrrrso,' Sweetie replied.

'Come. We'll catch some passengers at the Goyash–Kalikapur crossing. Nolbata businessmen, Ishannagar egg-sellers, Harhibhanga firan-sellers, Balumati scrap-collectors. Come, my strong one.'

The horse lifted his neck from his master's shoulder. He could tell, it was time to go.

It was market day at Goyash though by afternoon, the crowds would be gone. It was not an evening market, not like the one at

Islampur Chowk. Those who'd been shopping would be now be ready to go home. Per head, each passenger would pay from 5 to 7 to even 10 rupees for the ride. Businessmen tended to not haggle with fares.

There was another reason why Khodadil wanted to go to Goyash. He wanted to see how far the tar work had progressed. Having refused the compensation, Dilu was in both high spirits and low. If he had signed for the money, he could have got a set of strong wheels. Bought molasses and oilcakes for his horse. Even fine rice bran from the Biswas House at Chokjoma.

Sweetie went over to the carriage and stood in place before it, without any prompting. As if he knew exactly what had to be done when. Confronted with such a noble intelligence, Dilu's heart suffered a pang and he was moved to tears: 'This horse is, in truth, half-human. Always ready to carry my household on his back. Never turns away from pulling the carriage. Never arches his back, never sticks his hooves into the ground to say "I can't go on any more, Dilu." '

At Jagannath Das' Adi Annapurna Sweet Shop, Dilu bought a huge packet of hard molasses. Today his four-year-old daughter Nuri was not with him. He was devoted to her. He would have her sit at the front of the carriage. That's where she'd recite her alphabets. He had two sons, the elder one was in the fifth and the younger in the third. In Dilu's words, his daughter didn't know how to 'wan-fan'— that is, she hadn't learnt English, didn't go to school.

Sweetie pranced about his daughter, played with her.

Dilu taught his daughter a big secret. To make a horse trot, you have to recite a rhyme. Dilu taught his little girl the rhyme, a rhyme from the Battle of Karbala:

O *dear horse, my Dulduli O*
Go *fast now, now go slow*
To *the Tungi's city we have to go.*

Nuri would say:

O dear horse, my Dulduli O-O-O
Go fast now, now go slo-o-o-o-w
To the Tungi's city we have to go-o-o-o-o.

And then ask her father: 'Where is the Tungi's city, Bapu-ji?

Good question. Where exactly was that legendary city? In the Ishaan corner, or in the Nairrit? In fire, or in air? As they rode along, Dilu pointed his whip roughly in the direction of Harirampur ghat and said, 'Who knows, dear? Must be that way. That's where the road reaches the city.'

'That way to the Tungis?'

'Yes, my little mother.'

'You're sure?'

'The horse is sure.'

'Sweetie's sure?'

'Yes.'

Today when they arrived at Goyash, Dilu was a bit taken aback—it was totally deserted. Then at Bakultala, at Tabarak's shop, he heard that Nandi-babu had died, the owner of Nandi Stores. Hence there'd been no market today, out of respect.

Should he go back with an empty cart, then? Or should he catch some passengers from Matilaltola? He had to go home for an hour or two in the afternoon—he did so every day. He hadn't taken the money, and today he was dreading a bout of trouble with Sunabhan. She always spoke of his honour. Well, hadn't his refusal been an act of honour?

Dilu also saw, incredulous, that yes, tar had indeed been spread on this part of the road. The roller had smoothed it out. The black road, like a monstrous python, now lay before him, its mouth gaping with hunger. The sight of it made Dilu see red. In his mind's eye he could see the rabble of rickshaws descending upon it, like a flock of mud-scrabbling snipe. The rickshaw pullers, just like those birds—picking their food off the mud, the pitch. Leaping upon his horse from every side.

Instead of clicking his tongue as usual, Dilu suddenly whipped Sweetie in rage. The startled horse gave a leap and yanked the cart so hard that the packet of molasses fell to the ground, and a dog ran up at once and began to devour it. The packet stayed there, left behind. On one side of the road was resting a hooded jeep for hire. Dilu's ears grew red at the sight of it.

Khodadil felt as though the horse were pulling him off to Hell. As though he would fall. As if it was not a horse but a horse-jinn pulling his cart. It threw down my daughter's favourite food—and this is a creature I trust to play with her!

'Stop, stop,' shouts Khodadil. But the horse doesn't slow down. Then Khodadil remembers that it must be dying of thirst—it wanted to get back home to its midday meal.

'Wait, wait, dear Swootie. Good things come to those who wait. Khoda will send you a platter full of food. Don't you remember how Hazrat Isha prayed? Say al-Hamdo, Swootie! Bloody creature won't listen, O Lord. O Rasul, grant this creature patience, I pray you.' Khodadil tried to calm him down, lovingly rubbed his feet against the horse's belly. But the horse raced on; then after a sandy patch, the wheels slipped, the cart turned over and Khodadil was hurled into a ditch.

Khodadil climbed out, and thrashed his horse. Then left him and the cart behind, and walked back home. As soon as he arrived, he lost his temper again. It was a Sunday and all three children were home. Sunabhan had placed a sand-bottomed clay pot on the earthen stove in their courtyard. And he got at once the sound and smell of roasting gram. What audacity is this, Sunabhan! Giving Swootie's food to the children! Have you no shame!

'Wife?'

'Yes.'

'What are you roasting?'

'Just two fistful of grams, Nuri's father.'

'Why?' Dilu roars. In the scorching Chaitra heat, red dust devils swirl around him as he stands there on the briefly unpeopled road.

'Oh, moneylender's shit-eating woman, you steal my Tiger's food, you sinful bitch. I'll bring a second wife just to fix you. You dare to steal the gram? I spit on you, I whip your beautiful face. You, a witch! You'll eat my horse to death!'

'Be quiet, Nuri's father. I've heard you've donated money to the government? Why? If my children cry for food, should not I feed them with the gram?

'No, you won't.'

'Why did you give away our money?'

'Quiet, Sunabhan.'

'Why will I be quiet! You steal from us to do your comrade shit. Showing *prestige*! And my honour—won't people see that!'

'See! What is there to see!'

'Everything—they see everything. Some *prestige*. This road is my home, my household. Not even a curtain! If I need to birth again, where will I do so? Such love for the horse, and what about the children? Aren't they hungry? Won't they eat?'

'No, they won't.'

'Of course they will.'

The hot red dust seemed to swirl into his mind and cloud his senses. Grabbing a shaft of firewood, he beat first his wife, then his two sons. A few crumbs of gram were stuck to the corner of Nuri's mouth. She had never seen her father so inflamed with rage. Fear and disbelief made her eyes grow wide. She could not believe he would hit her too. She tried to raise a hand to stop him, to hold him back.

In her black tearful eyes, so like the horse's eyes, there swam only deep love. Nevertheless, the stick rained blows on her tiny back too.

As soon as he struck Nuri, Khodadil heard his horse arrive. Dilu ran over to him on the road that ran through the house, embraced his neck, closed his eyes, raised his face to the heavens and screamed.

Sunabhan and the children couldn't stop crying.

That night there was no moon in the sky. Khodadil could not sleep. Every night, around midnight, his daughter left his wife, crossed the road and came over to sleep beside him. Though she was so little, she was clever. She'd cross the road carefully, wait for a while if a herd of cows was crossing. Stop in case a cycle rang its bell.

Sunabhan applied warm mustard oil to the wounds on Nuri's back, ensuring that she did so in full view of Khodadil.

Now the brain-fever birds had begun to call. A male–female pair. It was rumoured that one bird had lost the key to their home. So the male asked: 'You have it?' The wife bird, astonished, asked back: 'I have it?' Their calls made Dilu's heart ache. These two birds, they just don't stop. Suddenly he thought: Is something really lost? What is it? Keys? A bag of money? What?

Will Nuri not come to her father tonight? Is her back hurting so badly? Will she never trust her father again? Will she never go with him to town? Never recite the alphabets sitting on the edge of the cart? Never ask again how far was the Tungi's city? Inside his chest will there only be this heartrending neigh, rearing its head in deep lamentation?

Suddenly the dazzling headlights of the jeep on hire sped across the courtyard-road. Nuri's eyes were blinded. The horse roared like a lion. Nuri, dazed, cried out pitifully for her father and then was crushed to death—the jeep ran over her and raced away. The horse ripped off its tether and tore off in a mad gallop after it.

On the courtyard-road, the child thrashed about from side to side, then spluttered up blood, then died. People streamed out of their homes clutching lamps. The horse wandered into a small forest. Its roaring cries, like bolts of lightning, set atremble a star in the sky.

The red road, thus, in black, inched a little closer.

II

By the time the red road was completely black, Dilu had finished his adult-literacy course. Newly literate Dilu had been well taught the first letter of the alphabet by his daughter Nuri. Dilu had thought the black python's back would at most be criss-crossed by rickshaws. But he had never imagined that the Majumdar-babus of Chawk would start a transport service with demobbed army jeeps. A rickshaw trip cost 15; a horse-cart trip 20; but a jeep trip cost only 3 or 4 rupees per head. Who, then, would Swootie compete with? Soon after the army jeep came Nanda-babu's Trekker.

Dilu had no choice but to start shared trips too. Even then, if they could, people preferred the jeep or the Trekker to his horse and cart. Even the rickshaw, once in a while. How cheap could a horse-cart trip be anyway? Three rupees a head? So 15 or 18 rupees per trip. That meant five to six passengers per trip at least.

Dilu sat in his cart and nibbled the end of his whip. Sometimes he manages one trip, sometimes not even that. Say, the passengers are about to sit in his cart, but then the jeep arrives—off they all go at once. Only an old man left behind.

'Get down, uncle. Swootie won't go.'

'Why not, son?'

'One passenger won't feed my horse. What will I keep, and what will I spend, tell me.'

'Well, Khodadil, then you'll just have to carry me home. I'm not getting off.'

'What a great thing you've said, Gokul-kaka!' said Dilu and spat on the road, narrowing his eyes in despair. Then thought to himself: Man is such a traitor. This same old man had fallen at my horse's feet when his wife was dying of diarrhoea. Cried: 'This horse is a compassionate creature, a creature of God.' Khodadil and his cart had rushed his wife to the hospital at the dead of night.

And today that old man was laughing and saying, 'Throw away this horse, Dilu. You can't feed him, you're starving it to death. Go, go sell it off at Chandni Chowk.'

'Such unkind words, kaka! Get down, get down right now. Go, go to the jeep—don't have to sit here looking like a nawab. Go—or I'll drag you down myself.'

'What! A mere cart-puller and you dare to speak like this? Hey, boys—who's there?'

Five rickshaw-wallas rushed over and almost began to beat Khodadil.

At least three tangas in this area had been put out of business as soon as the road was tarred. One tanga-wala was now pedalling a rickshaw. Not that it had increased his earnings significantly. Nobody could compete with the jeep, neither man nor forest animal. And Sweetie—he couldn't even go back to the forest—the poor thing had forgotten the way.

That night, from Motilaltola, on the homeward journey, Khodadil's cart was empty. This was the first time that he felt alarmed. Finally, it seemed, that Tiger Dulduli's days were numbered. The Battle of Karbala was over. Old Gokul-kaka had been right—Khodadil wasn't angry at him any more. Instead, his rage turned to that forest-forgotten animal, thumping its hooves on the ground and trying to shoo away the mosquitoes. The wife had not lit the evening fire as she did, the smoke from which usually drove them away. Come winter, the creature wouldn't get its usual jute firan-wrapper. Why had the eldest son placed a lamp near its feet? Its light shone on the creature—its eyes clouded over and watery, its legs grown thin, its ribs clearly visible. Yet Khodadil could not stem the tide of rage he felt against it.

It was because of this animal that Nuri had died—this incredible argument suddenly reared up in Dilu's mind and began to fan the flames of his wrath. He felt like killing the beast.

'My daughter ate your food—so I beat her. She died. And you stand there crying today? I can't bear it!' Khodadil picked up a piece of firewood. Rushed at the horse to beat it, but stopped in his tracks. He couldn't do it. He burst into tears.

Next day, Swootie's cart fetched only 15 rupees. Dilu got just one run with one passenger. Then he came back home. The horse withered away even more. This vile and worthless creature, this mute beast—it had no food to eat.

The throne of Allah in the sky seemed to swing from side to side. The maulavi at the maktab said, 'You are committing a sin, Khodadil. You gave your daughter qurbani for the road. Now don't kill the good lord's creature too. Either ply your tanga in Lalbag city, tanga city—or sell the horse.'

Dilu came home. Now the road no longer seemed a courtyard. Rather, the courtyard had become the road. The home and household too had become the road. And the road become a python. And Nuri's little face kept flashing through his mind.

One day, the road contractor came home. This was the man whose jeep killed Nuri, yet the road had not punished him in any way. Khodadil had no option but to join with his horse in his daily-wage work. Near Harirampur Ghat, a stretch of the road was still untarred. The tanga was needed there, to carry loads of broken bricks for road-building. What irony!

Never had Dilu imagined that his beloved cart would carry bricks, and that his beloved horse would have to pull such a load.

One day's work earned Dilu 80 rupees. It has been so long since he's seen so much money. Once upon a time, there'd been much money, much earning and spending. The money felt warm in his hands. He glanced at Swootie's forlorn face. That sad face, nothing seemed to make it happy any more. As though it were withering away in grief. Does it remember Nuri? He felt a pang of love and pity for the animal. He thought of spending some of the money on oilcakes, molasses and gram. Give it a good meal, make its belly full. He went to the shop and stood in line. Then, suddenly, a crazy thought occurred to him: Dulduli was his enemy.

He rushed out of the shop and bought some mutton instead. Back home, the whole family sat down so happily for dinner. The half-fed horse, standing on the other side of the road, stamped his hooves in fear and shooed away the swarms of mosquitos. From his eyes streamed drops of sacred zamzam water.

Suddenly, Khodadil's eyes fell on Dulduli. He could not eat any more.

'What happened, O Nuri's father?'

'There's something in the meat. It's Swootie's hair! See, son, isn't that so?'

' No, no, Father, there's nothing there. Eat—eat.'

'It smells.'

'Of what?'

'Of Swootie. It's been so long since I've given him a bath.'

'Keep your madness to yourself—let the boys eat.'

That night, Khodadil sat up alone, unable to sleep. Early every morning, when the Fajar namaz was read, the horse would neigh softly. These days it no longer did. These days Khodadil and his tanga no longer went off to work until late in the day.

Today Khodadil made a double trip. Today he earned 40 rupees. Today he bought gram. But stopped just before buying some oilcakes. And, strangely, the next morning he said, 'Sunabhan, why don't you roast some gram.' Sunabhan was astonished—she stared speechlessly at her husband for a few moments, at his face grown so hard with cruelty.

Khodadil took the roasted gram, left the cart behind and set off with Swootie. He walked for a while, then after Sadarghat he finally climbed onto its back.

The weak horse, its back bending under Khodadil's weight, bore its master along. The whip fell on its back, lashed its legs. The good lord's creature started and strained. Slipped and fell twice or thrice. Khodadil beat it mercilessly every time. Through the whipping, this most obedient creature patiently laid its back down before its master. Didn't utter a sound. Didn't stamp its hooves in rage.

It was afternoon by the time they reached Lalbag. To Mirza Nanihal's, in Chandni Chowk. Nanihal was amazed at the sight of Khodadil on horseback but happy, in the end, to be visited by his friend. Khodadil held out a handful of roasted gram for the horse, and said, 'Keep this creature, Mirza. I can't feed it no more. Pay me what you can. If not, keep it for free. I'm off.'

Swootie did not eat the gram. And grew restless as Khodadil began to walk away. Then, in Lalbag, the city of tangas, Swootie got food again and began to pull the *tourists* here and there.

No horse any more. But the name Ghoradil remained.

One night, when the brainfever birds called again, Khodadil remembered Nuri's voice:

O dear horse, my Dulduli O-O-O
Go fast now, now go slo-o-o-o-w
To the Tungi's city we have to go-o-o-o-o.

Ghoradil-Khodadil, in the grip of a terrible agony, held Sunabhan to his chest.

'You have it, Sunabhan?'

'Have what, husband?'

'My Nuri. My Swootie. Where have you kept them, wife?'

'I haven't kept them. You're the one who left Swootie at Chandni Chowk.'

'No, I haven't left it. I haven't kept it.'

'Why do you lie? You didn't leave it?'

'Give it all back to me, wife!' wailed Khodadil and burst into tears.

Sunabhan was bewildered by her man's childlike sobbing. She stared at him silently for a while. Outside, the birds continued to blame each other for losing the key. Then Sunabhan, as if she had finally found the key, whispered with suppressed excitement in her husband's ear: 'Yes, husband, there is a way to get it all back. Pray to the Qased. Nuri will come back to my womb.'

'Qased?'

'Yes, the Qased of Karbala. If a man finds no horse, he becomes one himself. Be your own horse, calm your grieving soul. Tie the bells round your waist. The anklets round your feet. Fill your body with force, Ghoradil!'

'Ghoradil—you call me that? You take your husband's name upon your tongue?'

'Yes, I do, Nuri's father. The road's not left you man any more. And I can't call you Allah, can I? But if I call you Qased, then what harm is there? You will bring me news. You will tell me what lies in my belly. You will pray to the Qased.'

Sunabhan's words make Khodadil's eyes slowly shine with happiness. Yes, he would become Qased. Feel in his body and soul the beat of Swootie's gallop. He would become the horse, and run wildly all the way to Karbala.

Daily wage-labourer Khodadil now understood that life was, in truth, a wondrous horse dance upon this road. Dulduli used to dance with Nuri. The memory of that dance now slowly encircled Khodadil. On the road stood Khodadil, Dulduli's bells tied round his waist. Dulduli's anklets tied round his feet. The horse's tiny bells tied round his upper arms. A marigold garland round his neck. He bent low in prayer in the direction of the mosque. Then stood still on the road, deep in thought. Where does this road end? And where does it all begin? Will his road end when he reaches Karbala?

As Qased sets off, all the villagers—young and old, men and women, boys and girls—come out to see.

'What are you praying for, Sunabhan?'

'I've whispered it to Qased, aunt.'

'You should light lamps at Nabiji's dargah . . . One lamp for Husayn, one lamp . . .' the women burst into song.

And the man-horse leapt onto the road. Half-man, half-horse, he danced for a long time to the rhythm of the jingling bells.

Then Sunabhan walked up to him, put a small tin box into the cloth bag on his shoulder: 'Here's some mehendi paste. Smear it on the white patch on Swootie's forehead. Ask for his blessing. Ask him: "I want to hear from your mouth: Will Nuri come back to us?"'

Bearing aloft the prayers of the villagers, Qased sets off for Lalbag-Karbala. With him went the mehendi, their good wishes. Their pleas to light a lamp. As if he had just now wed Sunabhan. As if she will stay awake all night, waiting for him.

He'll have to run eighteen miles. Qased never stops. The messenger-horse of Karbala never slows down. In a little while, though, the not-very-strong Khodadil was exhausted. The sky grew dark with clouds, lightning flashed and a storm burst upon him.

O dear horse, my Dulduli O
Go fast now, now go slow
To the Tungi's city we have to go.

If he doesn't reach Karbala, how will he bring back the news? Rain and wind and storm—can anything stop Khodadil now? So many times he slipped in the mud, so many times he rose and ran again, no matter how tired he was—he ran on and on.

As soon as he reached Karbala, the rain stopped. And the old city shone in the sunlight. People streamed into every nook, every cranny. So many tangas, rattling to and fro. A few, still waiting for passengers. Nanihal was not at home—he had gone out with Sweetie.

Where's my Tiger? Will he recognize me? The wife's given me mehendi, to smear on his forehead. How is he now, the creature of Husayn? Where is he now, the dishonoured and defeated and discarded horse of Karbala? But—who discarded whom? After all, Tiger was still ferrying people up and down the streets of the old nawabi city. In that dusty city, the creature, like a shadow, was still pulling its cart.

Whenever he hears a neigh, Dilu grows restless, looks up and down the street.

I've brought it, my son—I've brought mehendi for you. I've come to see you. I've come to dance with you. Give me rice, my son—feed me. I'll give you gram, I'll give you oildcakes, give you *fine* bran, molasses and chapatti, khesari and the blue flowers from the peas—I'll give you everything. Take me, my son. Come, my Swootie, come. Answer me. There, he's calling—there! All the way from Karbala, he calls, O Lord!

The swirling crowds pull along the mad Qased with them. In a frenzy, Khodadil pulls out the little tin of mehendi and smears the red paste all over his sweating face. Before his eyes float the newly wed Sunabhan's mehendi-red hands. In the heart of Khodadil's desire springs up a Milky Way. A horse neighs loudly at its end, far off in the distance. Nuri races down to her father, running so quickly. And with her, playing and prancing, runs a black horse.

Swootie-ie-ie-ie-ie, Dilu screams, and falls amid the throng. The feet walk on, walk over him. Khodadil lies there, his forehead streaked with mehendi, with blood and thirst and sweat.

Far away, tied to a cart is a black horse. A white mark on its forehead. At the sight of the fallen man, it neighs loudly. Stamps its hooves. Begins to struggle wildly. But cannot break free. Nanihal Mirza pats it gently, strokes its side, cannot understand what has upset it so.

Then, something strikes Mirza and he unties the horse. And the solitary, pierced-with-arrows horse of Karbala, begins to run. Eighteen miles is nothing to him. But Swootie, galloping through the streets of Lalbag, does not know who he is looking for. Only his eyes are gleaming, shining with an incredible hunger for the road.

The Measure of Land

When it was time, my sister and I would set off to collect dead leaves. At other times, at the crack of dawn, we'd visit the gardens of the rich to steal flowers. The two of us went to the fields too, to gather up the few sheaves left over after harvesting. We'd pick the fruits fallen on the road—wood apples, boheras, guavas. And sell them.

Back home, the sheaves were husked to separate rice from chaff. Then the grains were steamed. Then spread under the sun to dry. Then Ma would visit the neighbours, use their dhenkis to pound the grains, and finally serve us the rice she had collected thus. Rice that my father, my sister and I ate with such delight.

We had tin plates, but they were dented. So we ate not on plates but on banana leaves or lotus leaves. Lotus leaves grew in the master's pond. If Baba and I were lucky enough to be asked, then we'd spend the whole day standing in the water, collecting the leaves. The leaves were used for wedding feasts. The father of the bride or groom would pay us for them, maybe even let us eat at the feast. We'd always bring some food back for my mother and sister, but in secret. For we were always scared. Scared of our hosts. Scared of those who owned the paddy fields. Scared of the master. We had no land of our own, you see, no property, no trees, no climbing creepers, no flowers, no fruits. We were landless.

For seven generations now, we are landless. The villagers used to call us *refugee* though neither our ancestors nor we had come from Pakistan or Bangladesh. And whether our ancestors had truly been landless—of that nobody had proof. It's just that people said so, and it is better we believed so. So we do. Baba, of course, said that he could vouch for at least three generations; they at least had not owned any land. Baba's grandfather had not owned land; neither had mine.

So, for a long time now, we have not owned trees. Not owned fruits or flowers. All our ancestors, it seems fair to deduce, had been gatherers. Gathering flowers-grains-fruits—that was our profession. And if we were sure that no one was watching, we even managed to steal. Some things. Such as flowers.

If we were caught stealing flowers, the master's servants would at most box my ears, nothing more. My sister would be spared. I had grown used to having my ears boxed. We were Patuas, painters. But our father could not practice our painting trade. Our surname was Chitrakar, picture-maker. We were partly Hindu, partly Muslim. Not any one thing in all.

One day, Baba and Ma were talking. 'I say, Bhanumati,' Baba said, 'Badarpur is home to Lord Krishna. It's not such a bad place, after all. My heart says we should become *permanent* here. There are the lords, the masters, some *bandobast* might be arrived at. Suja Choudhury and Banka Majumdar—both are rich, well known. If any one takes pity on us, we might even get some land to live on. Bankim Chandra Majumdar, or Banka-babu. People also call him Babumoshai. I've heard he owns about 200 bighas. And Suja Choudhury, or Sujauddin Choudhury—he owns 250. If either of them give us even 2 kathas to live on, we'll be saved.'

'Will we?' Ma asked.

'We might, one never knows.'

'How?'

'If we get some land, anything can happen. Given a chance, a half-and-half painter can become a full-and- full Muslim. If I have to become another low-caste, say a Koibarto, I'm ready for that too. At least the *refugee* stain will be removed. Don't want to live with that disgrace any more. In this half-and-half life, I've found neither Krishna nor Khoda.'

'Have you spoken to Banka or Suja?'

'It's hard to get to them, Bhanumati. But I've talked to Suja's manager, Moslem Talebar. He told me I've got a chance.'

'A chance at what?'

'There are 3 bighas of land in Bhelu's name.'

'Bhelu?'

'Bhelu Sardar, the Choudhury's dog. I said: "Say that I am Bhelu Chitrakar. Can't that land be mine?" Moslem said, "When the dog dies, I'll give you that land, Chitra-kar. Be patient." '

We had next to no idea about land. We had built a hut on a strip of Babumoshai's land. But it was rumoured that the land was not legally his. Hence, some day, it would be taken over by the government and be entered into the records as theirs. And we would have to leave.

'Listen, Bhanumoti,' Baba said, 'the dog is old. You should do namaz every day, keep roza. If you do this with full devotion, Badarpur's Bhanu Chitrakar will acquire a good name. And Suja Choudhury will donate his dog's land to a man. Talebar asked me to follow the path of Khoda. Suja holds namaz gatherings in his house. Talebar's said he'll take me along. Next week, I'll learn to use the plough. I've spent two days now at Tinbigha. Don't you want the smell of farming to seep into my skin?'

'Yes I do.' Ma replied.

'We'll have our own land. Our own trees. Our own creepers. Our own leaves. Our flowers. Our fruits. Our home and household will fill up to the brim. Don't you want that? Our *own* land. It's been a dream for seven generations. Only that dog—that dog needs to die.'

Baba went off to Talebar to ask how old the dog was. The two of us, brother and sister, went off to collect dry leaves. Ma was a rice-husking, chira-making woman. If she husked one maund of rice, she got paid a ser and a half. She worked all day long, husking rice in other people's homes. She always smelt of barn and husk, of rice-soaked water. Hence my sister was named Bashomoti Chitrakar. She too was supposed to become a rice-husker like Ma. She had finished Class Two and gone up to Three; I was in Five.

Baba weighed only thirty-seven and a half ser. Talebar said: 'You won't be able put on weight if you don't become a ryot.' Hekim Jaynuddin gave Baba a bottle of Baghdadi tonic and said: 'Become a farmer. You'll put on weight. Seven generations with no land—that's not a good thing, Chitrakar. Moreover, whether your land is legal or not, at least you won't be a *refugee* any more. Stick like glue to Suja Choudhury's gatherings. He has land in the names of his dogs and birds. You're a human being. If you can, use the manager to transfer some in your name. The government's measuring land now, doing their survey. See if you can get your papers quickly. Say the namaz every day. If Khoda wishes, you'll get the land you pray for.'

The words 'the land you pray for' stayed with my father. With help from Talebar, he became a part of Suja's namaz gathering. He'd become a full Muslim and then start farming—such was his dream and desire. It gripped him entirely. He began saying the namaz. And to keep an eye on Bhelu, the dog. How old is he, when will he die— such evil thoughts haunted him daily.

He had evil thoughts, and then begged forgiveness for them from Khoda. Slowly, the painter became a farmer. Suja taught Baba how to farm, how to use the plough and sickle and scythe and spade.

Not that people had much faith in my father. A thirty-seven-and-a-half-ser painter has abandoned the gods and goddesses of his ancestors and now prays five times at Suja's namaz gathering so that he can become a Muslim farmer—that's all well and good. But such a lightweight chap, can he really work on a farm? Apparently, during the rains of Ashadh and Bhadra, he's lost a ser or two more!

The next Ashadh, Baba's weight went down to thirty-three and a half ser. Hence Suja had to arrange for a smaller plough. Hence Madhu Bhaskar, the carpenter, and Kaba the ironsmith had to be sent for.

A small plough. With a small edge. And a small blade. Suja sent Isha Muhammad Khalifa to Godhanpara, to buy a pair of oxen as small as deer. The oxen were really like deer, deer without horns. Kaba made a small iron blade and Madhu a small wooden handle for it. All through the neighbourhood was spread the incredible story of the painter turned farmer. Baba's gaze, though, was fixed on the dog. Until it died, nothing would be realized. For a dog's land to become a man's—this was not so easy, after all.

'How much longer do I wait, master?'

'Good things come to those who wait, Chitrakar. Remember, I've struck out Bhelu's name and given you 3 bighas of fertile land. Within my *ceiling*, there's no land more fertile. Not only will you get some land, you'll get some of the best!'

In the meantime, the government had begun its land survey. Tents were set up here and there. Preparations were made for a new kind of land measurement. The air began to throb with 'Bargapatta', 'Bargapatta'. No other word could be heard.

If Bhelu stayed alive, then a group of enemies would no doubt tell an officer: 'Sir, this land' s not in the name of a human! Bhelu Sardar's no man—he's Suja's dog!'

The government clerks in their land-survey tents would be astonished: 'A dog!'

Thinking such thoughts, he walked back home under the scorching Chaitra sun, having tilled 3 bighas of land in Nayadihi, that painter-caste man, weighing thirty-three and a half ser, who had changed his surname to Sardar—Bhelu Sardar.

The deadly heat of Chaitra, so hot it could melt the skull and the brains within. On top of that, it was Ramzaan month. A month-long fast. Without water. The not-Hindu, not-Muslim Chitrakar was keeping roza. His tongue was parched. Today was the twenty-second day of his fast.

A Saturday. My sister was now in Four, I in Six. On Saturdays, my sister's school ended at one. Instead of coming back home, she clutched her books and slate to her chest and went off to Suja Choudhury's house. She knew that, after working on the land at Nayadihi, Baba would come there, his plough over his shoulder. She loved Baba very much. Such a little girl, but already so clever. The apple of her father's eye. She knew, even in Class Four, what tormented her father so. My sister was so very beautiful—even in cotton pants and a frock, she looked as lovely as a princess. Her tiny heart always ached for her beloved father.

That day, around half past one in the afternoon, Bashomoti arrived outside Suja's drawing room. At once, the dog leapt up and began to growl like a tiger. It had a chain round its neck, and was a terrible terrifying beast. Even Bashomoti knew it had land in its name. Its fur was golden, like a lion; its tail was coiled.

There was no other dog as frightening as this anywhere in the village. It should have been named Tiger. One could not look into its eyes for too long. One's blood turned cold. One's limbs began to tremble.

Suja loved it more than life itself. At the sight of the animal, leaf-gatherer Bashomoti's face grew pale. Though he was chained, Bhelu was not to be trusted. He had been known to snap free of his chain and leap upon visitors. Rip off chunks of their flesh. Many in the village had been bitten by him. All his victims had, of course, been poor people. Now, not a beggar came close to the house for fear of Bhelu. It was rumoured that tiger blood ran in his veins.

Bashomoti had rushed over impulsively, without much thought. Now, terrified, she brought out some half-eaten bread from a pocket and threw it before the dog. Bashomoti did not know that Suja had forbidden strangers from offering Bhelu food. What she had just done was as good as a crime.

It's possible that this unusual occurrence surprised even the dog. He stared quite suspiciously at the bread. It lay near the threshold, on the veranda of the drawing room, about five or six inches away from Bhelu. Would he cross the threshold? One couldn't quite tell. His tail was coiled, not given to wagging. So one could never know if he was ever pleased about anything. A strange kind of beast was he.

'Aa. Bhelu, Aa,' called Bhashomoti, her tender voice quivering in fear. It was obvious she was still a child, or she would never have thrown him the piece of bread. Never dared to call out to him. What will happen now?

Bhelu stuck out his neck and then lowered it to the ground, displaying a feeble curiosity about the offering. One did not know how long his chain was. Nor whether he would cross the threshold and come out all the way to where the bread lay.

But then he raised its head and licked his lips. For the first time. He who had never eaten a bite of 'outside' food—for it was forbidden by his master. Besides, he was always well fed and hence never hungry. Suja fed him with his own hands.

But Bashomoti was not meant to know, nor was it possible for her to know, all these things. No matter. Frightened, she had thrown the bit of bread. And now—Bhelu slowly crossed the threshold. Began to sniff the bread.

Just then Baba spotted Bashomoti and ran over to her. 'What are you doing, my mother! What a disaster!'

By then, Bhelu had begun to eat the bread. It did not take him long—two gulps and it was gone. A bit of bread, swallowed whole.

But the man Bhelu was aghast. Dumbstruck. Terrified.

'You shouldn't have done that!' he said, his voice shaking, 'It is forbidden to offer the dog food. Even Suja's servants are not allowed to do so. Let's go, let's get away at once, Bashomoti!'

'It's not like I gave it poison, Baba. It was growling, so I gave it some bread.'

'You shouldn't have! But, wait—what did you say? Poison? No matter, let's go.'

And without another word, Chitrakar and his daughter walked back home.

But in his mind had taken root the idea—poison. That day, when he sat for namaz, he could not control the tremors that shook his body.

Bashomoti went up to Five, I to Seven. Baba carried on farming. We no longer went from garden to garden, gathering dry leaves. Ma used to light her kitchen fire with those leaves. Now Ma uses a wood fire. Baba has become a regular labourer on Suja's farm. He was now a namazi-farmer. By a stroke of good fortune, the land survey had stopped midway. If it hadn't, who knows what would have transpired. People said: 'The Nayadihi land, the one in the name of the dog, it's illegally owned by Suja. Chitrakar will never get it.'

Banka Majumdar had instructed Kaba to visit the tent-babu and tell them all about it. Kaba touched his Sunnahti beard and took an oath to do exactly so, to visit the babu and tell him that the 3 bighas in Nayadihi belonged not to Suja but to his dog. The government should take it over. Decide whom to legally lease it to.

'Listen, Babu, Chitrakar's a nobody. He's a *refugee*. An infiltrator in our Badarpur. He reads the namaz, it's true, but doesn't know the verses by heart. If you must give it to a pious man, give it to Dukhu Sikdar. Chitrakar uses a tiny plough, his harvest is minimal. Also . . .'

Then, one day, someone poisoned Bhelu the dog. News of the dog's death blew across the village like a sad wind. People said: 'Who knows who killed the poor dog! That thirty-three-ser Chitrakar's not a straight man.'

Across their minds, grief for the dog flit like a shadow, like clouds that darken the sky. They were surprised to know the dog had not died at home but near the pond by the paddy fields. Someone had taken off his chain. And fed him poisoned food. They were even more surprised to see Suja being so quiet about it. And happily letting Chitrakar live on those 3 bighas. They had assumed Suja would throw him out. They had thought that the loss of the dog would have been like losing a family member. That Suja would have despaired as if he had lost a child.

Since none of their imaginings came true, they grew somewhat downcast and slowly trickled back to their homes. And silently rained curses upon Chitrakar. 'Man doesn't think twice to kill even a brother for some land. I guess a dog is nothing in comparison.'

Those who'd attended the namaz congregation at Suja's drawing room said that Suja kept repeating: 'Who gave Bhelu poison? How will I know?' That is all he could do to express his grief. His voice had grown low and weak.

The land survey resumed.

Some still said that if only Chowdhury got proof . . . he wouldn't let the dog-killer go.

Some said, 'A dog's land going to a man—why does that upset you so?'

Some others said, 'Banka-babu has fit Kaba to a plan—wait and watch, why don't you?'

Our life thus took such an unexpected and strange turn. We had never imagined that owning land would be so difficult. To tell the truth, we had no idea whatsoever about land.

I could sense that something was eating away at Baba. An endless discomfort. His eyes, dogged by a deep confusion he was fighting to conceal. He no longer wanted to talk to us. Ma too had grown haggard over-night. No longer smiling and cheerful.

'Did you really poison the dog, Sardar?'

Once upon a time, Ma used to refer to Baba as Chitrakar. Of late she had begun to call him Sardar.

'No, Bhanumoti,' whispered Baba, 'I did not.'

'Did not it die of poison?'

'Yes. It did.'

'Then?'

'Don't ask, Bhanumoti. Don't ask. Be quiet. We've built our hut on Banka's land. He's already said, "Get lost, wherever you can." Or he'll come here and smash our house to bits. But where do we go now, wife? Should we go to Nayadihi?'

'The 3-bigha land? You want to go there?'

'We've nowhere else to go, Bhanumoti.'

'Then let's go, Sardar, it'll better than this. It's on the edge of Khalasipara, not too many houses nearby.'

'Not too many? More like none at all. That place is far, far away. And all the houses set far apart, scattered here and there. The fields are full of howling jackals. Being chased all night by the dogs. You want to live there?'

'Yes.'

Before Babu-moshai could evict us, we left. Came away to 3-bigha Nayadihi. Built a new hut. Baba even built a little shed for the cow— an almost adult cow he managed to get hold of. Chitrakar's life slowly grew replete. We had our own trees, our own creepers, our own flowers and fruits. The pumpkin creeper on our hut's roof burst forth with flowers. Flat beans grew aplenty. Bottle gourds and runner beans and cucumbers began to ripen on the frame. The purple flat-bean flowers blossomed, as did the ones on the brinjal plant. Green papayas grew on the tree. We owned a guava tree. A custard-apple tree. The berry tree in the courtyard was covered in flowers. Bees buzzed everywhere. Flocks and flocks of parrots descended, such an incredible green. A yellow bird came. Came the long-tail bird, the mynahs and the tree-pies. The spotted pigeons. Even an owl flew in one day and perched on the roof. Sparrows pecked at the grain in the courtyard. Baba planted saplings of litchi and mango. We became householders.

The land survey was advancing at a swift pace. It was not a one-day job. One year stretched into another while they measured 1 mauza after another. In the meantime, the Chitrakar home and hearth grew full with fruit and flower, peace and prosperity.

One afternoon, Suja sent for Baba. An urgent summons.

'See, Sardar,' he said, 'I want this land to be made legal, have papers. Nabi Mollah and Talebar Moslem, my manager, will go with you. You must tell the survey-babu that you own that piece land—that I've donated it to you because you're my sharecropper. If Kaba the ironsmith brings up any talk of the dog, you tell the officer: "Can a dog farm that Suja will *registry* his land to a dog?" Tell the officer: "Actually, the dog and I have the same name, so some people have just made this up." When you say all this, Nabi Mollah, the most pious man, the most religious man, will speak up on your behalf. What he will say I have already taught him. Go, get ready. Also, Sardar—I want to try and be MLA in the next election. Understand? It's not good for an MLA to have land in his dog's name. Bhelu Sardar is not a dog—he is a man. Talebar has drawn up a certificate in your name, *backdated*. Don't forget that the history of land is always a crooked one. Land is a sinful thing. Now, go.'

I went with Baba to the officer's tent. Reading off the plot register, the babu asked: 'Who is Bhelu Sardar?'

'It's me,' said Baba, standing up and folding his hands. A man trembling in fear, a man without land for seven generations.

Kaba saw Baba and lost his temper.

'That's not Bhelu Sardar,' he spat in rage, 'That man's Chitrakar. Bhelu is dead. He was poisoned.'

'Bhelu is dead!'

Dumbfounded, the babu stares at Baba, then at Kaba.

'That's what I'm trying to tell you, babu. This is Bhelu Chitrakar—not Bhelu Sardar.'

'You say someone poisoned Bhelu—who was it?'

'Chitrakar.'

'What!'

'Yes, sir. A helpless creature, and this man killed it.'

'Helpless creature?'

Nabi Mullah sprang to his feet, clutching his beard.

'Who are you?' the babu asked him, 'What do you want?'

'I'm a religious person, babu,' Nabi replied calmly, 'I perform namaz five times a day. Listen to what I say. Suja-babu donated this land to Chitrakar. When he began to pray namaz, Suja-babu began to call him Sardar. Suja-babu did have a dog named Bhelu but there is no proof that Chitrakar poisoned the dog. Chitrakar was made a farmer by Suja-babu. This Chitrakar—now Sardar—farms at Nayadihi, on the 3 bighas he got, using a small plough, small oxen. He's built a hut there, lives there with his family. The land is over the *ceiling*. Whether you acknowledge Suja-babu's donation or not—that is up to you. But you must admit, babu, that a dog cannot till the land. A man, weighing only thirty-three ser?—maybe, just maybe he can. Somehow or other, his hands can push the plough. If need be, he can push with his whole body. No matter—he can still farm a crop.'

Nabi Mollah's word set off a furore outside the tent. The rivalry between Banka Majumdar and Suja Choudhury was known to one and all. And had split the village in two. Hence, the furore soon escalated into fisticuffs. And then a most terrible thing happened— one of Kaba's supporters struck Moslem Talebar with his umbrella. A deep gash appeared on his forehead, and blood began to seep in large drops down his face.

What a dreadful brawl! Baba began to tremble even more. He didn't know what to do. The survey-babu stopped taking notes and shut his register. His chair and table were in danger of being knocked over. The commotion was not going to be an easy one to subdue.

Kaba's men kept shouting: 'If he's such a great farmer, why was the dog poisoned to death?'

'You'll be cursed, just you wait,' shouted somebody else. 'Cursed! That hand that touches the plough will wither away with leprosy— I'm telling you!'

Baba's chest began to hurt. He sat down slowly. He understood that he had committed a crime. The death of a land-owning dog is no simple matter. That golden dog, the one fed bread by Bashomoti, the one she used to go back to sometimes and feed it this and that.

No matter—no decision was arrived at. The land-survey record was closed for the 3 bighas, the small plot they called Te-Bigha. When and how that record would be completed, and what the *ceiling*-babus would decide— Bhelu Chitrakar could fathom none of it.

Bhelu the dog acquired more fame after his death. Death by poison was a mournful tragedy, and many of the villager's minds had overflowed with grief. Chitrakar was an outsider, he could never be dearer to them than the dog. It had been the dog of Badarpur, it had even had three bighas to its name. Some strange man came out of somehere and killed it off with poison. So greedy was he for the land? Ha Khoda! Can one kill another creature like this?

II

Stage by stage, the survey moved on, and the officer-babus took their tents from one field to the next. Fixing the land ceiling and determining the leases—this was their task. But it was not easy to do. More often than not, the babus were discovering plots of land bequeathed to birds and beasts. In the case of Bhelu the dog, it all grew even more complicated.

One of the officers was a man called Subrata Kanungo. He was an amateur writer, had written the odd story or two. He thought of Bhelu Chitrakar as an *interesting* character.

Subrata-babu sent for Chitrakar. 'Since everything about you is of a smaller size, the task I have for you is also a small one. You'll have to carry the survey chain. I'll take the boat to Nidhinagar Bhatshala. When I set off, I'll be going upriver. You walk along the bank before me, pulling my boat along by its tethering rope. Then—I'll see what I can do.'

I saw Baba pulling the boat, pulling the rope and dragging along the survey chain. My thirty-three-seer father, how desperately he wanted to be a farmer.

'I'll feel I own the world, babu,' said Baba as he dragged the chain, 'if I own that plot of land. If I can't own that land, how will I ever know that all the world is mine? This land is mine, this woman, this map, these numbers on the map, these children, this hut and this courtyard. This tree. These leaves and creepers. These fruits and flowers. I had made all this with my own two hands—isn't that so, babu? Only then do I fell that this earth belongs to me. My ancestors could not—but I will.'

'Pull hard—pull harder, Chitrakar. Pull the chain. Only then will we start to measure your land.'

'Yes, babu,' says Baba, struggling to breathe.

'I like you, Chitrakar. You're a man of the earth. This earth will indeed be yours. Come, place the chain on your land. Start to measure. And those shouting on and on about the dog—I'm not interested in them. Let them see how hard you've worked to get your land.'

The crowds had gathered at Te-Bigha, it overflowed with people. Nabi Mollah had come too, and now waited patiently on the side. Bashomoti, unable to bear Baba's struggle, began to cry softly. Large tears rolled down Ma's cheeks. I stood there, unable to say a word.

By the time the measurement was done, it was almost evening. Once every edge was marked by the chain, Baba stopped and knelt down for a namaz. Perhaps he thought that the namaz was his last resort. To turn painter to a farmer. In truth, Baba had lost his mind. Before he could complete his namaz, he began to cry.

Then, ending his prayer, he stood up, turned his face to the sky and, slapping and beating his breast, began to perform a strange and awful mourning. Kanungo could not remember if any farmer anywhere, any landless man, had ever screamed so hard. The *public* too were amazed. They began to say: 'He killed the dog with poison, so he's mourning now.'

Bashomoti, frightened by her father's frenzy, ran over to him in the middle of the field.

Clutching her father with her little hands, the eleven-year-old girl shouted, 'My father did not poison Bhelu. It was Suja Choudhury! God knows, Kaba-chacha. Khoda knows, Nabi-kaka. My father did not kill the good lord's creature!'

The villagers realized it was the truth—Bashomoti was not old enough to lie. And they were all amazed.

One evening, just after his namaz, from his prayer mat itself, Suja had thrown a piece of poisoned bread to Bhelu. And said, 'Eat, Bhelu. If you don't die, Chitrakar won't get the land. I'm giving your right away to a man. Go, Chitrakar, take him off his chain, chase him away to where the animal bodies lie.'

That Baba chased the poisoned dog to its death, to its dying breath. That sin and that scene is what drove Chitrakar mad in the end.

Next summer, when Baba went to plough his land, he saw, far off in the distance a dog, huge and golden haired, glowing like a lion. And he cast his plough aside, and began to run after him, from this side to that.

I wanted to burst into tears.

O Lord, land is no little thing, is it?

Simar

Sukhobas did not have a single hair on his chest. His body seemed cast in iron. Iron does not sprout grass. The lord had not given his chest the soft, wet and fertile soil that was necessary for hair to grow. Rather, it seemed to be the arid plains of Karbala. In it reigned the incredible Simar. In that iron city, it was Simar who was lord. The thought of it broke Sukhobas' heart. The Muslims believed that Simar too had no hair on his chest. It was Simar who didn't let Husayn drink a drop of water, who pinned him to the ground and then cut off his head.

How cruel this kafir country is, my dear,
Poison in plenty, but not a drop of water.

All the Jarigans were full of his cruelty. Husayn's infant son cried for a drop of water. Just a palmful to drink. Husayn's throat was parched. But Yezid didn't send water—he sent Simar bearing weapons instead. Yezid too had no hair on his chest. How pitiless, how cruel, how merciless was his heart! Looking at his own chest Sukhobas would wonder: Then, am I Simar?

Sukhobas had just stepped into his youth. Growing tall and wide, like a demon. The muscles in his arms bulged like the body-builders', hard and proud. His legs, like the trunks of the banyan tree, straight and strong. The soles of his feet, flat and full and huge. His footprints in the dust as though of a beast. No shoes in his size could be had at the shops. They had to be made to measure by the cobbler. And his vest? The measuring tape fell short—his chest had expanded beyond it. Good lord—what kind of man was this!

Sukhobas bursts out laughing. And thinks: if he'd been furry like a bear, people would have called him Adam, respected him. The Muslims say: Adam, alaihis salaam, the first man, the first human being. And yet here he was, doomed to be Simar instead!

Dadima, his maternal grandmother, stroked his chest and said, 'Where is the hair, oh my dear? O unfortunate sinner! This marks you out as Simar's kin. A cruel line.'

Eighteen-year-old Sukhobas was as strong as a twenty-eight-year-old. A moustache grew and flourished on his lips, yet not a hair grew on his chest. Hair grew on his legs, like a dark stain, but his chest stayed pure, empty, white. Was white the colour of sin? Was sin the colour of emptiness, nothingness? Such thoughts made him cry. Made his eyes sparkle with tears. 'Dadima is scared of me, disgusted by me.'

Everyone took to calling him Simar. The name Sukhobas was almost entirely forgotten.

Then, one day, he was old enough to be married. But his father knew he was still a boy. Just because he was tall and strong, they all mistook him for a man. Dadima said, 'Bring a devout girl for him. Pious. Menstruating. Calm.'

The search began for a suitable bride, but Sukhobas, 'the abode of happiness', was not happy at all. All day long, he stayed away from home, fled about who knows where. One afternoon, as soon as he got back, he came over and sat beside his grandmother, his head hung low.

'Where have you been all day?' Dadima asked.

'Horses. Cows. Buffalos,' whispered Sukhobas.

'Understood,' said Dadima, bursting into peals of laughter. 'Whose horses?'

'Lebastulla's horses. Barkat's cows. Chaharuddi's buffalos.'

'Good. How much did they pay you?'

'Four for the cows and the buffalos, total eight. And ten for the horse.'

'You don't bother to study. Chase after cows and horses instead. How will you be a proper man then? '

'What will I get by being a proper man, Dadi? I am Simar—I am the sinner. You told me so yourself.'

'I was just teasing you. Can a true Muslim ever be Simar?'

'Yes. Yes, he can indeed,' howled Sukhobas. 'Farsi-sir in school, Sadek-maulavi, calls me a bullock. Always finds faults with my speech. Abuses me, calls me Black Mountan, calls me Simar. Lifts up my shirt to show everyone how hairless my chest is! Now everyone knows I'm a bad person. I'm not going any more. I've pushed and pulled my way up to Class Eight. And I've learnt enough. No more.'

'Yes,' Dadi nodded, 'it's enough. Don't go any more.'

'I'll graze the cattle, tend to the horse. Plough the fields. Work as a farmhand. A Muslim's education should be religious education. Reading the Qur'an, understanding it word by word. Instead, I went it seems to Simar school. There's no God in what this school taught me. No Heaven, no Hell either. I'm too old now. All the others are so much younger. I'm no good there. There where even the bloody teacher makes fun of me, unbuttons my shirt and—' Sukhobas began to sob.

'Get married, my dear,' said Dadi, rubbing his back, 'She'll help you find your God.'

Sukhobas wasn't paying attention. Because soon after he suddenly said, 'Tell me, Dadi, women don't have hair on their chest either, do they?'

'Women are wrought from tenderness,' said Dadi with a smile, 'they're creatures of compassion. But Simar is a man.' And, then, after a pause: 'If you love your wife, the lord will pour kindness into your heart. You're not Simar at all—that's a big lie.'

Sukhobas tucked his face into her lap. 'Make me a Muslim, Dadi,' he cried, 'It hurts, Dadi. It all hurts so much.'

Sukhobas began to learn the namaz. Began to attend the maktab-madrasa. But he was not good at learning things by heart. If some verses he managed to recite, some others he could barely remember. By the time he'd learn the end, he'd forget the beginning. In time he began to notice that, one by one, all the worst students from his old school were slowly getting admitted to the maktab. The brainy ones weren't too inclined to join. Not that one or two good minds weren't present, the ones who'd been too poor for high school. Those ones, over time, fell in love with the Qur'an so much that their communities glowed with pride. Then the light of God seemed to ripple in sacred waves over their eyes and faces, make them seem as precious as angels. They looked so beautiful that when you glimpsed them you felt as though you'd bathed in the waters of Mecca. It's true.

Taher-saheb was a qari, a reader of the Qur'an, and his recitation was melodious indeed. Sukhobas took off his shirt and asked him, 'See Qari-saheb, am I Simar? Do you think so too? Or is everyone else lying to me?'

Qari-saheb burst out laughing. 'Your chest is like Simar, true, but not your face. Yet, oh my son, even today you couldn't learn the Surah Fatiha!' Then, assuming an air of great mystery, Qari-saheb drew closer. 'Who are you really?' he whispered, 'I *don't know*. Ha ha ha.'

Qari-saheb was in the habit of using one or two English words in his speech.

Sukhobas understood that, in the Muslim world, no one had the answer to the riddle of his true self.

Two days later, Qari-saheb said, 'The maktab's rife with politics, Sukhobas. The village is divided. *Very complicated* situation. Only the Lord knows which side you're on. Is it wrong to call you Simar—or is it right? I just can't tell right now.'

Sukhobas went home. And found his father and uncles engrossed in talk of his marriage to Zahida, the daughter of Giyasji, the maulavi at their village maktab. A widower, he'd come to live in Sukhodohori village five years ago with his only child Zahida and a poor orphaned nephew, eleven or twelve years old. The nephew, Isha, studied at the maktab. Older now, he stayed with Ibrahim Ansari in the next village and walked back home after class. No matter.

Giyasji was not an exceptionally qualified maulavi. But he was quite well known as a teacher. The problem they now faced lay with him. For some time now, there had been a conspiracy afoot to apply for a government grant that would enable the promotion of the maktab to an Aliah madrasa. The secretary of the maktab, Saiphulla Mandal, wanted to his brand-new son-in-law, the FM–passed Quddus to run the maktab. But to do so, Giyasji needed to vacate the position. Giyasji, of course was FM-passed too while Quddus was still studying. Inshallah, he would acquire an even higher *diploma*. News of this was spread far and wide by his father-in-law. Besides, after completing his BA Part 1, Quddus had been to Uttar Pradesh, to study theology. On the other hand, Giyasji was not even a matriculate. Hence, it was appropriate that a *committee resolution* be passed, appointing Quddus to the post .

This maktab was nine years old. For the last five years, Giyasji had been running it on meagre wages donated by the villagers. Removing him, a good organizer, from the post, would stain the holy place with sin, wouldn't it? If his staying meant no money from the government, let it be so. The villagers would support him as they always had, donating money and rice and wheat and jute. If the maktab remained a maktab and did not become a madrasa, let it be so. Giyasji was not to be removed.

Two opposite schools of thought divided the village in two. One side simply refused to understand how vital was the acquisition of Quddus for the greater upliftment of the maktab. They loved Giyasji very much. While there were many who saw only too clearly the stealthy nepotism and skulduggery running rife in the prophet's house, the secretary's supporters were no less active or vocal. Saifullah had even won over a poor villager with the promise of making him the newly upgraded madrasa's bell-ringer *peon*. That villager's extended family was a large one, all very wily and rich. Only that man was very poor, able to do not much more than recite the prayers every Friday. Because of all this, the maktab was now aflood with waves of dissatisfaction. Something was bound to happen. Any day now, the maktab was due for an *inspection*.

In the middle of all this, there arose talk of Sukhobas' marriage. Giyasji had agreed to the proposal. Zaheda was eleven. A slim-slender girl, but already breathtakingly beautiful. A very sweet girl. Her skin the colour of gold. Studied in the maktab, and lived with her father. Some arrangement needed to be made for her. For reasons of his survival, it was imperative that Giyasji find a good household in this village itself to marry her into. Or he might end up losing his job. If needed, Sukhobas' family could lend their might to his cause. If needed, even fight on his behalf. That's all right, then. Understood, Sukhobas?

Sukhobas had been listening to his father and his uncles, and their words began to fill his heart with a kind of happiness. Zaheda's sweet and smiling face kept flashing through his mind. As did the helpless face of Giyasji, her father. Giyasji had grown old. Zaheda was his daughter from a second wife. His first and second wives had been doomed—they'd both died before him. He had a daughter with his first wife. She was married now, living with her husband. After a long, long time, Giyasji had married again. Zaheda was the daughter from that second marriage.

The second wife, Zaheda's mother, died when Zaheda was four. Two years after that, Giyasji and Zaheda came away to Sukhodohori. Everyone knew how badly he wanted to marry his daughter to someone in Sukhodohori itself, and then live out the rest of life here. He had no desire to return to Mograhat. He had a bit of land there, but he'd sell it off. And if someone got him married again to some elderly woman—Giyasji woudn't mind that either. In Sukhobas' family itself, there was a husband-abandoned wife. There was, slowly, some talk of such a match as well.

Sukhobas already thought he'd become Giyasji's son-in-law. While the rest of them were engrossed in conversation, Sukhobas went into his younger sister-in-law's room and picked up her *transistor* from the table. His older brother Arifat had married last year. His chest was covered with hair; his wife was full of mischief. Whenever she laughed, her eyes sparkled flirtatiously. And Sukhobas would feel shy and embarrassed. She laughed now, and he leapt away, out onto the veranda. Her laughter pealed through the air behind him. Sukhobas walked on quickly, out onto the road. Switching on the *transistor*, he turned the volume to full and pressed it to his ear. The radio sang:

I'll talk to the twinkling stars
up in the sky so far away,
if you don't want to come and talk to me

Sukhobas walks along, listening to the song. A huge moon hangs in the sky. Moonlight floods the path before him. Seems to bewitch him. Sukhobass walk brought him close to the maktab. A tall two-storey structure. The ground floor home to the external students, the maulavis and maulanas. They lived downstairs and studied upstairs. Classes went on till 9.30 a.m. Of the students, 70 per cent were girls. About 40 per cent of all the students went to the local junior high school at 10 a.m. for their 'regular' education. Hence the maktab was a 'morning' one, and the high school 'day'. The remaining 60 per cent studied only at the maktab; they did not receive any other schooling.

Sukhobas was now quite close to the maktab. He was yet to pray the Isha namaz tonight, the one that was prayed before midnight. It was half past ten. The path, deserted. Suddenly he heard the angry voice of Sobhani-khatib coming from a ground-floor room. He must be talking to the other maulanas, discussing the *hadis*. He would pray the Tahajjud—the midnight prayer. Then go back home to bed or sleep at the maktab itself. 'Switch off the radio, Sukhobas,' the khatib suddenly roared, spotting him in the moonlight, 'Son of a Muslim. Studying the Qur'an, yet playing such dirty songs so close to the maktab—don't you fear Allah? Forty years of prayer destroyed by one filthy song. Who but a descendant of Yezid could do such a thing? Why not—you're Simar, after all! If I had the *power*, I wouldn't have let you set foot in the maktab. Disgusting!'

The window slams shut. The radio stops. Sukhobas was certain that deep within his heart someone was waiting. Someone trapped inside and listening to the song. Sukhobas turns the knob on the radio. But no Arabic voice from the distant Arab land sang forth. Nor hymns in praise of the prophet from Dhaka. Suddenly he was overcome with the urge to throttle the khatib. At that moment, he felt he was indeed Simar. He rushed home as fast as he could and began to pray the namaz. His whole body shivered, as though he were running a fever.

The wedding night. Earlier in the evening, the bride and groom had sat in the courtyard, on chairs placed side by side. Eating the sweets and sherbet and water that was offered to them. The groom took a bite out of a roshogolla, and the rest of it was fed to the bride. Zaheda kept casting sidelong glances at Sukhobas. The young saree-swaddled girl looked as beautiful as a kolabou. Sukhobas was wearing a black woollen skull cap and a pair of white, crumpled pyjamas (made of *Japani terrycotton*, from Bangladesh). On his feet he wore leather sandals with criss-crossed straps. His socks were white, and already lined with dust. A khadi handkerchief was tucked into his pocket. And his face shone with cold cream, as though slick with sweat. The bride was being fed water from the glass he had sipped out of, as a sign of their shared life ahead. Giyasji was giving away his daughter to Sukhobas. 'Through good times and bad, I have held her to my heart. She is still a child. But she knows ten of the thirty parts of the Qur'an already, word for word. And she is a virgin. Make sure she suffers no indignity, my dear boy. Her breath smells as sweet as the angels. Never hurt her. Love her, care for her, make her happy—I wish for nothing more. Her life and death are now in your hands. Her good fortune, her ill-luck, all in your hands. The ground beneath your feet is now her paradise. Zaheda, O my mother, from this moment Sukhobas is your world. Your companion for this life, and the next. Your partner in every happiness and sorrow. Never disobey him. Give him whatever he wants as soon as he wants it. No matter how hard it is for you, never say no to him.'

The *hadis* says, even if your husband is aroused while riding a camel, you must fulfil his desire there itself. But Giyasji could not bear to speak this instruction aloud; the words stuck in his throat. For Zaheda's breasts were not full moons yet; her chest not yet flooded with their moonlight. Hayez, her monthly cycle, had not begun. Her body was still tender and raw. Even her bones were yet to fully harden. All this needed to be said too. But he could not. For he was a father. So he said nothing. Then, after a few moments, he said: 'Whatever your husband desires, whenever he desires it, you must fulfil his wishes. His every wish is your wish. His body is your body. His mind is your mind. One soul, one life. And your happiness is our happiness.' Then he stopped, his voice cracking with tears. The sight of him moved Nadira, Sukhobas' abandoned aunt, to tears too. She'd been standing on the veranda, with the other women, listening to him speak.

The wedding night.

The bride and groom went into their room. Someone or other bolted their door shut. Around midnight, an anguished female voice rose in a scream and then fell silent. All the women in the house rushed to the door and began to call Sukhobas. There was no answer. All was silent within. Then, the sounds of a struggle. The women glanced at each other and grew embarrassed. Quietly unbolting the door, they went back to their own rooms.

The sun rose. Sukhobas opened the door and stepped out. Sat on the veranda, leaning against the wall. His face puffed up. His eyes hibiscus-red. His white lungi spattered with blood. Everyone rushed into his room. Zaheda's mouth was stuffed with the edge of her saree. The bed was smeared with blood. And Zaheda was dead. The saree was pulled out slowly from her mouth. Her eyes stayed open. Cold. Still.

Zaheda's funeral rites took place around noon. Then her burial. Then, under Saifullah's instructions, the police came. Accepted a bribe from Sukhobas' father and went away. When the police questioned Giyasji about the whole affair, he said nothing. After much insisting, all he said was, 'It's all fate, sir. I don't know what happened. Does anyone kill their bride on their wedding night? And both of them, such children.'

A wave of disquiet rippled through the village. That disquiet heightened when the police came away with nothing. But because Giyasji continued to stay silent, the gravity of the situation slowly began to fade away from their minds.

That evening, Sukhobas paid Ratan Nandy a visit. 'Give me your new horse, Nandy-babu,' he said, 'let me try and tame it. Teach it to wear the halter.'

Sukhobas leapt onto the horse. The horse began to run, straight towards Shiladihi forest. The sky grew darker. As they rode on,

Sukhobas bumped against a knot of vines tangled around a tree trunk and fell. The horse ran off somewhere. The darkness was not too deep—up in the sky, the moon was shining. The forest sky was obscured by branches and leaves. Moonlight seeped in through the cracks. A carpet of leaves covered the forest floor. The moonlight and the darkness mingled and melted. Sukhobas got up and began to look for the horse. The animal was nearby. He could hear the dry leaves crackling beneath its feet. All night, he played hide and seek with it. Heard him moving about, but could not catch him again. Finally, exhausted, he came to a mango tree. Lay down beneath it. And fell asleep. The night deepened. In time, the moon sank in the sky. All was dark. A little cold. A wind began to blow. Both the eastern sky and the forest stood still in that slowly lightening darkness. Slowly, the horse made its way back to Sukhobas. Sukhobas was still asleep. The horse nuzzled Sukhobas, breathed against his skin. Touched Sukhobas with its wet-warm mouth. Sukhobas' sleeping body gave a shudder. He woke up. Saw the horse's shadow and was startled. Was filled with an incredible fear. It was not a horse—it was Zaheda! Zaheda's death. A terrible form of that death. When Sukhobas had touched her, Zaheda had cowered just like he was now, and cried, 'Oh Khoda! Khodaband!'

II

Ashamed, Sukhobas could not bring himself to go to the matkab any more. After the incident, he had been there only once. The maulavis hadn't spoken too kindly to him. And the students had stared.

In fact it had been Giyasji who had sat with him, explained the lesson to him. Been kind. 'Study hard, be devout,' he'd advised, 'Fear Allah. Become an imam, maybe a maulana. If you have committed a sin, beg for Allah' forgiveness. Cry in repentance.'

Sukhobas came to realize that his place in the community was slowly shrinking. At the same time, of late, he had also felt as if the villagers were finally forgetting the whole unfortunate episode. Zaheda had been an insignificant creature. Such deaths were not entirely unheard of. He'd spoken to his friends in secret. It was not uncommon for young brides to flee to their parents' for fear of their husbands and their demands. Sukhobas and his friends had often seen such girls silently running along the village roads, running away.

No matter. Seven months later, Sukhobas was married again. 'Get a lively one,' Dadima had said this time, 'A bold and strong one. Full and ripe. A young woman—not a girl.'

Dadima's instructions had been obeyed to the letter. Medina was bold and strong. Full and ripe. Fully woman. Fully feminine. Her father wove gamchhas, cotton towels. And was wretchedly poor. He'd come to this village selling his gamchhas, and taken the opportunity to arrange the marriage. A man with a good heart. He had no disgust for Sukhobas. The poor are usually possessed of good hearts, and are not too generous with their scorn. Besides, a girl's father can't afford to be snobbish. So, the marriage took place.

The wedding night.

It was summer. Sukhobas took off his shirt and sat for a bit on the veranda, enjoying the breeze. He also made sure he read the namaz. Finally, he went into his room. Medina was startled by the sight of his hairless chest. Not a single hair. A terrible emptiness. As soon as Sukhobas drew closer, she put her hand on his chest and implored: 'They all say you're Simar. Don't ruin me. Don't kill me. I know, even in the heart of stone there runs water. I will love you. Never hate you. Simar was a Muslim too. Will you love me?'

Sukhobas could not speak. That Simar was a Muslim too—this was the first time someone had told him so. The first time someone told him that water runs in the heart of stone. And the first time a woman spoke to him of love. He had never been able to speak of his sin. He'd been afraid, they wouldn't listen to him. They'd hate him. His heart now quivered with both joy and fear. 'I am Simar, it's true,

Medina,' he said, 'People's words have made me so. I stuffed Zaheda's mouth with her saree. Who knows what possessed me then! Do you understand? She was like a soft little bird, and I choked the life out of her. Can you believe that? Stuffed her mouth and . . .'

'I believe you,' said Medina. Then traced on his chest with her fingertips the three sacred letters: Alif-Lam-Mim. In her eyes shone the bright light of her deep and dense love. 'And then Zaheda stopped breathing?'

'No, no,' said Sukhobas, 'Not that. Not like that. Another crime stopped her breath. And that I can't speak of, my dear. She was awash with blood. The blood of sin. Alas, alas!'

Gently pushing away Medina's hands, Simar began to pummel his chest. Somewhere inside it, someone seemed to be wailing, lamenting 'Hai Hasan, Hai Husayn'. An inconsolable screaming. Like the Muslims who weep for their Husayn. Like the Shias at Muharram, sobbing for the deaths of Karbala. That same grief echoed in these cries.

'I can't bear to remember her face, Medina,' he said, 'I just can't. How do I make you see how pure that face was!' He began to hit himself again, then placed his forehead on the pillow as though in prayer. Pressed down on it with all his strength while his body shivered and trembled. Pressed it flat beneath him. Then began to speak of his fear. About Nandy-babu's horse. About how the horse had got lost in the forest. Then come back at dawn and nuzzled him awake. The sound of the leaves. The moon. The darkness. The cold breeze. The taste of death on the horse's tongue. As if Zaheda had come back. Or some other terrible thing. The horse's sharp scream. The sky and Allah's forest, trembling. How awfully he had been punished that night! 'Nobody knows this, my dear. Nobody will understand.'

Medina traced three letters again, this time on his back: Kaf-fe-re. Kafer. Then slowly rubbed them off with the edge of her saree.

Medina's father, Gophurjola, was supremely content after marrying off his daughter. A poor gamchha-weaver, he'd go from one village to the next, hawking his wares. Sometimes he'd cross the border, wander into Bangladesh. Struck by a whim one day, he took along his wife—and then never came back again. The news trickled through to Medina who sobbed softly for a while. Then she told her husband, 'I have no one left in this life but you. If you spurn me, I have no place to go. Don't leave me. I will give you whatever you want, no matter how difficult it is for me.'

The words made Sukhobas' remember his first marriage. Remember all that Giyasji had said. But Zaheda's face—that he could not remember at all. He wanted to see her clearly in his mind's eye. So many days since she was dead, yet not for a moment had he glimpsed her again. Why not? Why was there no image of her in his heart? Can Simar hold no picture dear? Or was it because Zaheda had been so pure, her breath imbued with the scent of angels? 'Try to remember,' Medina said, 'Think calmly. Meditate. Zaheda will come.'

Suddenly, one day, Sukhobas finally understood. Why would Zaheda come? Just because Medina said she would? Just because his new educated-right-up-to-her-*school-final*-exam wife said she would? Her belly cried no more for two fistfuls of rice. She was now with Allah. She felt hunger no more. When she was alive, when she walked the earth, when she lived in the world above her grave, only then did she need shelter. Why had Giyasji wanted him to marry his daughter and become their kin? He had no one. And Saiphulla would snatch away his job. Throw him out, render him destitute. So he'd offered Zaheda as bribe. But then?

Medina, too, in the same hope of shelter had glimpsed water in the heart of stone. Had forgiven Simar. Agreed to make love to him even in the daytime. Not make love. But fornicate. As soon as it's done, she gets up and leaves. Flings opens the door, walks out of the room and busies herself with some chore or other. If no chore awaits, then she picks up the broom and starts to sweep the house clean. Her face grim, humiliated, unhappy.

But no matter how hard it hurt, Medina will not die. The light of that promise can be seen shining in her eyes. Medina is a strong young woman. Will she understand?—no, she won't—how hard Zaheda had tried to fulfil Sukhobas' desires?

'Do you know how I killed her? Her mouth clamped tight, she lay there, enduring my torments. Her body, so cool and pure. Light, as a flower. Fragrant, delicate. In the beginning, she'd screamed once or twice. Like people scream for God when they're in trouble, or afraid—like that. Mumbled her prayers. Perhaps she'd thought the Qur'an's verses were powerful enough to transform her instantly into a full-bodied young woman. But Khoda could not save her. Then she screamed louder. I tried to stop her, stuffed her mouth with cloth. Then I realized that she was quiet. Cold. Not crying any more. That Zaheda was dead. But she had tried her best to fulfil his need. As was her sacred duty as his wife. Is that why Giyasji has forgiven me? Is that why the villagers have begun to forget it all? Is this the way of the world? Was Zaheda really such an insignificant creature? Does her death mean so little? I thinks so. Such things can happen to anyone—in fact they happen all the time. That's why Medina says, "Zaheda will come." If I meditate, she'll come. Not for two fistfuls of rice. Then why? For what? After all, it's not I who *planned* to kill her. I was Simar then. That's why I killed her.'

Innumerable hazy thoughts slowly set astir that ancient still mind, now weighed down by the burdens of life.

Medina was trying as much as her faith and faculties would allow her. Every night, at midnight, she would carefully create a suitably spiritual setting. Persuade her husband to concentrate and recite the Tahajjud namaz. Light incense sticks and say to him, 'Raise your hands to God and weep for mercy. Pray. Call Zaheda. She will surely come.'

No matter how hard he tried, Sukhobas never could see Zaheda in his dreams. The prayers didn't help. He couldn't sleep. At some point, he'd turn to Medina, partake of her body. Slowly, Medina's firm and full body began to overshadow the memory of Zaheda.

Every day, after reciting the dawn namaz, Sukhobas began to visit the maktab while the day was still hazy with darkness. Sat silently beside Giyasji. Then, as the morning grew, he'd touch Giyasji's feet in respect and slowly walk back home. He had no wish to study at the maktab. For Sukhobas, a glimpse of Giyasji filled him with as much virtue as a glimpse of Kaaba. Filled him with bliss.

Thus, life carried on.

One day, suddenly, Saiphulla managed to put his plan to work.

That day, a little before the midday Zuhar namaz, Sukhobas had been to visit Giyasji. Asked him, 'How do I get a glimpse of Zaheda, Abbaji? She doesn't come in my dreams, you see.'

'She will. She comes to me. She comes to me so often. Sits by me. Talks to me. Wants to be fed. After all, while she was alive, I never managed to feed her well enough. That's why she wants to be fed. For two fistfuls of rice, I came all this way, to Sukhodohori. It's hard to live off other people's charity, my son. See, Saiphulla's daughter still hasn't come with the rice. I think, from now on, I'll just eat at your place. You can become my host, my shelter. The *secretary's* charity is a terrible thing. And Sayra, his daughter, the one who brings my food every day, is an impudent girl. A bit too smart. Wait. I'll show you. Can't speak of it to anyone else. It's outrageous!'

Giyasji scrabbled about in a box beneath his cot, fished out a piece of paper and handed it to Sukhobas, 'Look! Look what's written on it!'

A stunned Sukhobas reads a line scrawled in an immature hand: 'I will marry you, Master. Your, devoted Sayra.' Sukhobas' eyes grew round with astonishment. 'See?' said Giyasji, 'What kind of girl she is? Though I suspect it's not Sayra who's written this. It's someone else. What do you think?'

Sukhobas was inclined to agree. These words didn't sound like Sayra. Some ulterior motive had inspired this note. Sukhobas looked out of the window and saw Sayra approaching, dressed in a salwar kameez, her dupatta flowing behind her, carrying a covered plate of food for Giyasji. Sukhobas leapt up from the cot. 'I'll keep that note, Abbaji,' he said, 'I want to show it to Medina. Then, when she thinks it right, Medina can send for Sayra. Have a word with her. I'll go now.'

Sukhobas rushed back home. And there, just as he was about to speak to Medina about the letter, one of the neighbours, a girl, rushed in panting, 'Saiphulla's men are killing Giyasji! Sukhobas-bhai, why do you stand there? Grab your stick, and come ! Hurry!'

Sukhobas' father and uncles ran off at once to the maktab. Sukhobas grabbed his stick and followed suit. When they got there, they found Giyasji surrounded. Being manhandled, pushed and shoved. Apparently Giyasji had tried to disrobe Sayra. This was not the first time; there had been earlier attempts. The salwar kameez she was wearing had saved her honour today.

Sukhobas' arrival resulted in a pause in the agitation; then it resumed with greater intensity as soon as Sukhobas' stick landed with a resounding crack on Saiphulla's head. None of the other men had sticks. Saiphulla had a couple of strong men in his gang, some even as wide and tall as Sukhobas, but they were all unarmed. The blow made Saiphulla bleed quite heavily. The blow, like a bolt of lightning from the stick of the indomitable Simar, stunned not only Saiphulla but also all the other men. The disturbance was set to escalate but was not allowed to. Sukhobas and his relatives came away, bringing Giyasji home with them.

Soon after, Saiphulla retaliated with a harsh decision: he was going to call a *meeting*, and dismiss Giyasji from his post.

Sukhobas for his part showed everyone that little note and said it was all a ploy. 'My father-in-law is innocent.'

The village was split into two clear camps. All the headmen from the neighbouring villages got together, held a court. Such a session was known as a 'twenty-two court', for twenty-two headmen participated. On a specified day, with all of them as witness, Giyasji would have to stand in the masjid and swear upon the Qur'an that he had never laid a finger on Sayra. The slightest stain of suspicion on a maulavi's character would bring about the instant end of the maktab. For most of its students were girls.

The day they all agreed upon was a week away. Giyasji, already driven out of the maktab, sought shelter with Sukhobas. His head was now always bent low in shame, never to be raised high again. As though he were nodding off to sleep. His eyes, too, remained closed most of the time. As though he were sunk in mute meditation.

That day finally arrived. That day, Sukhobas had taken the new pair of cattle to the fields in Daulatdihi, to bring back the harvest. He'd planned to be home by afternoon. Giyasji was to appear at the mosque just after the Asar namaz. Hold the Qur'an and swear that he hadn't touched Sayra. There might be some trouble again, who knew, thought Sukhobas.

Such thoughts had already set his temper on edge. Then, fetching the harvest, he'd had to push and pull the cart through the mud. Tiny water mites had bitten him, made his whole body sting with their bites. His legs were caked in mud up to his knees. He was worn out with exhaustion. Panting. Occasionally gasping for breath. The cattle had refused to cooperate. Sukhobas was frustrated and furious, utterly at wits' end. When he finally got back home, he stopped the cart in the outer courtyard. His body was soaked in sweat. His eyes and face and chest, streaming with perspiration. His breath like an animal, panting.

'Medina!' he shouted.

Medina and Dadima were deep within the house, gossiping. They didn't hear him call, they were too busy talking and laughing. Sukhobas waited in the inner courtyard. The afternoon wore on. They must have gathered at the mosque already, he imagined. He began to run out of patience. Such disobedience was surely against the scriptures!—Medina seemed to be ignoring him, not giving him his due attention. He called out to her again, this time even louder.

'Simar's come home, Dadi,' whispered Medina with a wink and a smile.

'Oh, Simar's back, is he? Go, my child. Get ready. Cool him down. Go, go now.'

Sukhobas heard these words. And was shocked. So, behind his back, even his family thought he was Simar! Made fun of him! Gossiped about him! He thought they loved him but in truth they loathed him. Thought him to be a base creature, not a man. It was too much to bear. Suddenly, within him, roared Simar, that Simar, the heartless one. Medina was still inside, perhaps tidying herself up before coming out to meet him. Sukhobas grew enraged, Simar grew even more ferocious. His legs were caked in mud, his body itching and burning from the insect bites. Yet Medina had kept no water ready—none to clean his feet, to bathe his body, to wash himself clean. By the time Medina stepped out and stood before him, his mind was wholly in the grip of the beastly Simar. A Simar who's killer instinct was now baying for blood. Sukhobas no longer had any control over himself, over his past or present or future. Medina'd brought a pitcher of water for him. Only one pitcher? To cool and comfort him? Wash him clean? Soothe the insect bites? A terribly fury exploded within Sukhobas.

'Do you hate me?' he said.

'Hate you?' Medina asked, amazed, 'Why would I hate you?'

'It looks like that to me.'

'No. That's not how it is.'

'That's exactly how it is. You hate me. Abuse me. Call me Simar behind my back!'

'I was just teasing.'

'Teasing?'

'It was wrong of me.'

'And only one pitcher of water! Is this the *time* to tease?'

'I'll get you some more, a whole bucketful.'

'No. You don't have to. I'm giving you talaq. You leave right now.'

'What?'

Medina was stunned. Suddenly she could no longer recognize her husband. She had heard many stories of husbands giving talaq. Now she finally understood that talaq was a *hadisi* disease that afflicted men. It was *hysteria*. Like epilepsy, like malaria.

'Talaq!' declared Sukhobas. The next moment Medina rushed over and clamped a hand over his mouth. Sukhobas pushed her away, flung her to the ground. And shouted 'Talaq, talaq!' Called out to the neighbours, and said: 'Come, all of you! Listen, listen! I'm giving her talaq! Talaq, talaq, one more talaq!'

In an instant the courtyard was thronging with people. Medina was still lying on the ground, dumbfounded. Unable to believe what was happening.

Sukhobas' father rushed out with a stick and began to beat his son. 'Bastard! Yes, you are Simar. Swine! *Hot-temper* bastard! Witless! Wicked! Son of a bitch! Impotent! Showing off your manhood only to helpless, defenceless women. I'm going to kill you today!'

Sukhobas was thrown to the ground, beaten mercilessly. Blood began to seep from the edges of his mouth. The blows from the stick left red stripes down his back. Medina, still stunned, rushed over to her father-in-law, and grabbed his stick: 'Don't. Please don't. He understands nothing. Not even a joke, O Lord.' Then she covered her face with her hands and began to sob. Her cries rose up into the sky, raced all the way to Allah's throne.

III

Giyasji arrived at the mosque. Qur'an in hand, he stood on the stairs from which the azan was read. His limbs were trembling. He'd heard Sukhobas giving talaq. Seen it all. Seen Medina's keening cries rising up into the sky and speeding off to Allah's throne like a shimmering spear. Then he'd left the house, begun to walk to the mosque.

A huge crowd has gathered. Suddenly, among the faces, Giyasji spots Sukhobas. A light shawl wrapped around him, though it isn't large enough to cover all the signs of his revent beating. He looks like an ancient statue, tall and mute. A primitive man. Giyasji stares at him, and his limbs seem to tremble even more. He clutches his little Qur'an tighter, and begins to speak, his voice unsteady, 'My dearly beloveds, all you who gather here, I have done no sin. Touched no woman but my wife. Sayra is like my daughter. Let Allah save her honour and mine!'

Then, with shaky steps, he slowly comes down the stairs. Sits at Saiphulla's feet. Puls out a handwritten document from his pocket, and says, 'My resignation.' And then falls unconscious to the ground. Isha, his orphan nephew, rushes over and holds him to his heart. Cries, 'Uncle! Oh, Uncle! Uncle!'

The crowd disperses.

Giyasji returned to his lodgings at the mosque. Rarely ventured out any more. Sukhobas' family sent him food every day. But somebody else carried it over. Not Sukhobas. Why not? Because Sukhobas did not go back home any more. He had begun to live in the orchard instead, behind the house. An orchard full of mango trees, litchi and jackfruit, plum and rose apples. The fruits had all been plucked, but the bamboo scaffolding across their branches was still there. Sukhobas climbed up on the scaffold. Henceforth, that scaffold would be his bed.

Medina was a stranger to him now. Even if their eyes so much as met, it would be a great sin. Medina had nowhere else to go. So she carried on living in that house. Sukhobas could live in the orchard or wherever else he wished. The scriptures forbade them from meeting ever again. Medina was meant to have left for her parents as soon as the talaqs were uttered. But where were Medina's parents? She had nowhere to go.

Sukhobas was wiser now, his mind grown much sharper. He refused to let himself step inside the house. If he ever wanted to do so, he sent a message from his perch in the trees. And his brothers and his mother, they would come out to the orchard and spend some time with him. Bring him his food. But they failed in all their attempts to bring him back home. Sukhobas' voice had grown soft and deep, like that of a man bearing a great sorrow. 'Why are you so sad?' he'd tell his family, 'Don't cry. Everything will be all right. I can't let go of Medina. I can't live without her. That room in truth belongs to her. I have merely given her what was hers. And come away to the forest. After three months, I'll come back.'

In the forest, he had to endure the mosquitoes. And the fear, as he lay there all alone. He wished he could see Medina. Wished he could talk to her. But he had no choice. Saiphulla's gang was keeping watch. Near the outer courtyard, men could be seen hanging about beneath the gourd creepers, late into the night. Early in the morning, in the afternoon, even in the evening, they roamed about. Keeping an eye out for Sukhobas trying to come back home. Inventing excuses, pretending to seek a light for their smokes, they'd sneak into the house just to make sure he wasn't there.

His father could not bear this torment. He felt so sorry for his son. And just as angry watching him pine away for his wife. The old glory of this household had dimmed. He wanted his son to come away from the forest, come back home and be with them again. Medina was now the Lord's responsibility. Let her go where she wished. Let her die, even. Become a beggar. Become a prostitute. No one in this house could tolerate her any more. And Medina— thinking only of her mad Sukhobas, she carried on enduringd that life of snubs and slights, of endless unhappiness. She had realized that the mad Sukhobas, the cruel Simar, had fallen in love with her. It was for her that he had exiled himself into the forest. Spent his days roaming aimlessly down the village paths. But three months was no little time. Would he be able to last that long? At the dead of the night, wouldn't he ache for the touch of a woman's body? His relatives kept going out to him, coaxing and cajoling him to come back. But that man, who by the strength of his will alone lived in the forest—she was the only one truly on his side, truly his.

One night, in the heart of darkness, Medina walked to the forest and climbed up the scaffold. Gave her body to Sukhobas. Not a word was spoken. In such gifts lie the secret of another kind of spiritual power. That which runs deeper than the power of scriptural faith. That which Medina felt running through her body and soul. As she flung away modesty and honour, scripture and religion, Medina began to laugh. A strange and silent laugh. As though she had gone mad. She had no choice any more. No sense of right or wrong any more. No community. She was Simar's castaway bride. Worth no more than kindling for the flames of Hell.

On the scaffold, in the darkness, lies the lonely prisoner. Through the cracks in the canopy of leaves, he can glimpse the stars in the sky. See the moon. And he remembers another deep and dark forest. Remembers a horse. The dry leaves crackling beneath his hooves. Remembers everything. He waits now, his ears cocked, for the sound of approaching feet. The night grows darker still. He falls asleep. And he dreams an amazing dream. In a shallow pool floats a girl, like a half-dead fish. One of her arms is like Zaheda's, and the other like

Medina's. Sukhobas wades into the water. The hands reach out to him from its depths. How strange they are. They clasp his feet and begin to pull him in. Sukhobas struggles but cannot shake them off. Where does Zaheda want to take him? Sukhobas screams. And finally sees her. Oh, how horrible! One arm healthy and strong, the other thin, ghostly. Sukhobas' throat is parched with fear. That ghostly hand scrabbling for Sukhobas in the water. Sukhobas is terrified. He wakes up. Finds himself alone on the scaffold. And no sound of feet on the leaves. Sukhobas climbs down. Tramps over the dead leaves and comes, like a thief, through the darkness to the maktab. Crumples at Giyasji's feet and murmurs, 'Abbaji!'

Startled, Giyasji stares speechlessly at Sukhobas, stares at his face glowing in the light of the lamp. Reaches out and pulls him close. Holds him to his heart and says, 'You've come, after all!'

IV

Sukhobas' appearance made a shudder run through Giyasji. He seemed to have diminished somehow. No longer like a wild buffalo. Deep dark circles had formed beneath his eyes. 'Take me back home, Father,' Sukhobas said, 'I want to go back home. It's been three months and ten days. Please, do something about Medina.'

Giyasji had already given the matter some thought. 'But to whom do I marry her off?' he said, 'Who will marry her? Just a marriage isn't enough. He'll have to marry her, then feel sorry for her and then give her a talaq. So that you can wed her again. Do you have a friend . . . ?'

'No, Abbaji,' said Sukhobas, 'No one I can trust. After all, who knows what they have in their hearts. Friend and companion—you are everything to me. Tell me, won't Isha be willing?'

'Isha?' Giyasji murmured. Then sat silently in thought. 'All right,' he finally said, 'I think that's best. I'll marry her to Isha, purify her by his talaq. Then give her back to you. Isha is a good boy. He won't turn his uncle down. Go, now, and be at peace.'

Sukhobas went back to the forest.

The next day, Giyasji spoke to Isha: 'The very next day, early in the morning, you must divorce Medina. Utter your talaqs. Just that one night . . .'

Giyasji stopped speaking, and Isha silently stood up to leave. But Giyasji was not done with him. 'What happened, Isha? Don't you have anything to say? Are you not willing to do this? You will do as I say, marry that woman. Go now. But come to Sukhobas' in the evening. I'll be waiting for you.'

It was ten in the night by the time the marriage ceremony began. Isha arrived, dressed up as a groom. He'd even lined his eyes with surma. Worn a freshly washed kurta, scented with attar. His head bowed respectfully, he carefully pronounced every line of the vows. Giyasji himself conducted the ceremony. The courtyard was teeming with people. The bride and groom sat in the drawing room, facing each other. Hazak lamps glowed on the veranda, near each pillar. Every now and then, the crowds spilt onto the veranda, surged like a wave around them and then ebbed away. Sukhobas was nowhere to be seen. Giyasji assumed he was in the forest, lying alone on his scaffold bed.

Sukhobas was, in fact, standing just beyond the glare of the lamps, in the darkness near the bushes, and watching everything. This wedding was very different from his and Zaheda's. Sukhobas strained to hear the instructions Giyasji was imparting to Isha. But the crowd was chattering, the low hum of their voices and the scattered evening sounds didn't let a word of it reach his ears. It was a cold night. Sukhobas buttoned up his shirt. Drew his thick shawl tighter around him. Waited. Giyasji made his nephew drink some sherbet. Then held the same glass to Medina's lips.

Saiphulla's men were among the crowd. They too were watching everything. Giyasji brought his mouth close to his nephew's ears and said, 'Remember, you're a Muslim. A Muslim's honour is very strong indeed. You're not Simar—you're Isha. This night is your test. A Muslim always fights alone. Now, both of you, go inside, go to your room.'

Medina and Isha went into their room. Giyasji shut the door behind them, and then pulled a chair up to the threshold. Sat on it to keep guard. Giyasji was no longer that despairing defeated man; he seemed to have got a fresh lease of life. 'When I speak to you, Isha,' he called out from this side, 'you must reply to every word. Without delay.'

'Yes,' Isha replied from within. Softly. So softly that the crowds outside could not hear.

Slowly, the outsiders began to trickle away. They had realized that Giyasji would keep vigil all night. So there was no chance of sneaking a peek, or of eavesdropping. This mad maulavi had spoilt the fun. One or two boys and girls lingered, still hoping for a chance of a word or a glimpse. But Giyasji scolded them, sent them off. 'There's nothing to see here. They've gone to sleep now. You lot go home now as well. Go!'

They had no choice but to do as he said. Only a little distance away, in the house next door, at the window, two eyes stay awake. Nadira. Watching Giyasji, a true Muslim. She could not fall asleep.

'Are you all right, Isha?' asked Giyasji a little later.

Isha did not respond. 'Tell me, Isha!' Giyasji asked again, injecting a little warmth into this voice.

'I'm all right, uncle. But Sukhobas killed my sister on just such a night. Stuffed her mouth with cloth and took her life.'

'Yes, he did,' said Giyasji. 'But you will not lay a finger on Medina. You will prove that you are my blood. A servant of Islam. A man of the mosque. You are not Simar. Don't hurt the body of the one who is weak and helpless. Let not even a single drop of blood be shed.' Giyasji could not continue and began to sob loudly instead. Then, in a voice thick with tears, he cried, 'Oh my mother, Zaheda. My girl.'

At the moment, the scene inside the room was very different. Isha walked over and sat very close to Medina. Then, in one movement, he pulled down her saree from her shoulders. Medina said nothing, but her face grew pale and her words dried up in her throat. Then, suddenly, 'Yes, father,' she shouted, 'Here I am. Your Zaheda.'

Her cry startled Isha, and he regained his senses. Stepping back a few paces, he began to sweat in fear. And then shouted, 'No!' That impotent uncle. Poor. Starving. And weak. He who shouts 'Islam, Islam' just to fill his belly—no one believes in that Islam. I won't let Medina go. Won't give her talaq! Never, ever!

But he couldn't say any of this aloud. Looking into Medina's eyes, he just stood there, staring at her. The night grew longer still.

Suddenly Giyasji saw a hurricane lamp drawing closer, a lamp shining its way over to him through the heart of the night, a lamp hovering just a little above the ground. At first he hadn't been able to tell it was a lamp. Just seen a small circle of light. As it drew closer he saw it was a covered bullock-cart. And with it, a group of eight or ten men. Saiphulla's men.

'You've done enough sacrilege,' said Saiphulla, as he came and stood before Giyasji. 'Now, come. It's time to go. We've had a long talk with Isha. The two of them are leaving. You are too. The bus comes at five to the main road. These men will reach you to the bus stop.'

Once again the courtyard surged and swelled with people. Isha heard Saiphulla's voice and rushed out of the room. Giyasji was stunned. When a dam is on its last legs, straining against the weight of the water, then cracks begin to appear in its walls. And the water, through those cracks, sprays forth in long silver jets. Giyasji had not finished giving Isha all his instructions. But he had been lucky—

Medina was a highly intelligent woman. How swiftly she had acted, pretending to be Zaheda. Although even that had been in vain.

The crowds swelled even more. In the distance, the clump of bushes gave a little shudder. But no one noticed. Isha quickly climbed into the cart. Saiphulla's men dragged Medina out of her room, pulled her all the way to the cart. Medina began to scream, her face turned up to the sky. But not a single member of the family responded. No one rushed out to help her. Only Nadira screamed, in the distance, at her window, 'Sukhobas!'

The clump of bushes shuddered and shivered. But Sukhobas did not come.

'Go,' said Saiphulla, 'go quickly. A little more than six miles. It's not midnight yet. Now, who's going to drive the cart?'

One man, his head wrapped in a turban, stepped out of the crowd, sat in the cart and gave the bullocks a prod. Four of Saiphulla's men were to accompany the cart. One of those men forced Giyajsi onto it. Dumped him on a seat beneath its shade. One of the four was Dedar Baksh-maulavi, the other three were maktab students.

The cart raced along. After a mile spent in silence, Giyasji opened his eyes. A deep and terrible darkness seemed to have swallowed everything around them. From underneath the cart, the swinging soot-covered hurricane emitted a ghostly light. A light that struck the four escorts and made their shadows swing and sway. Made them look unreal. Giyasji stared into the distance, sought the line of the horizon. But could see nothing in the dark. Where were they going, in the middle of this terrible night?

'I never imagined,' he finally said, 'that Saiphulla-sahib would give me such an honourable send-off.'

'Yes,' said Dedar Baksh softly, 'After all, only the Lord can decide who is an honourable man.'

'I'm so glad you're all here with me.'

'Why?'

Giyasji did not respond. The cart bumped along. And soon they'd covered another two miles. Suddenly Giyasji began to recite an Arabic surah. A long verse from the Qur'an. He knew it by heart. A low sound, from deep within his throat. Now and then, he struggled to draw breath. Endless sparkling fountains entwined themselves around each word and exploded into the universe. Then, stopping for a moment, he turned to Isha. 'You say it too, my son. My son, Isha,' he said, his voice rippling with love and an almost divine adoration.

Isha, meanwhile, had been lost in the fragrance wafting from Medina's perfumed body. Been overcome with the desire to penetrate the very core of that body. Been overwhelmed with the yearning to see how far he could take the desperate urge he felt for her. But it had all been turned to nought. Now, suddenly, as his uncle spoke, he felt as though it was the Prophet speaking to him. And the sparkling notes of the surah seeped into his tender teenage soul. The world around them appeared ethereal, transformed by the beauty of the words, its melody. Isha began to say them softly too. Began to surrender to their divine spell.

'Give her talaq,' Giyasji reminded his spellbound nephew: 'One talaq for the one krosh we have covered.'

'Talaq', Isha uttered, his spell still unbroken. Then carried on reciting the surah.

'What are you doing, Giyasji?' Dedar Baksh was shocked.

Giyasji did not reply. But turned to the three students and said, 'Mizan, Maqbul, Idrish—you recite too. Recite the name of Allah.'

Their three voices instantly blossomed into a chorus.

'What are you doing?' shouted Dedar Baksh. 'You're scaring me. Saiphulla said . . . See, you've got to think of my job too . . . I mean, my responsibility . . . '

Giyasji paid him no heed. But carried on reciting, even more loudly. How remarkable a journey he had embarked upon. An ethereal, otherworldly migration, a journey away from all mortal desires towards happiness. Towards accepting life's every hurt and humiliation as though each were a drop of nectar. Towards leaving behind every grain of bitterness. He was replete with the surah's melody, his soul blossoming like a flower in the sound. Petal by petal, he unfurled and spread himself out, as though all the way to Heaven.

The cart bounced along, past the river. The waters echo the good Lord's voice. The sound washes over the men like a wave. At the end of the fourth mile, Isha uttered the second talaq.

Suddenly, Dedar Baksh leant closer to Maqbul, one of the students. 'Have you noticed the driver?' he whispered, 'I think it's Simar!' Maqbul looked up and froze, the words of the surah stayed stuck in his throat. Dedar spoke the same words to Idrish and Mizan. They too looked up, and grew frightened at what they saw. The four of them stopped walking. Despite what Saiphulla had said, they could not take another step. They turned away and slowly began to walk back home.

'Why did you stop?' Giyasji asked the driver, 'Come on, carry on. Two talaqs have been given. You heard them yourself. Didn't you? When you meet Sukhobas, tell him I gave all three. Only two miles left. And then you'll take Medina back. Isha and I will go away on the bus. You can do that, can't you? Come on, keep going.'

The driver gives a groan, a sound distorted by both grief and joy. An ancient, wordless and inarticulate joy. He hits the bullocks hard. They leap forward and begin to run. The surah recital begins again too.

A while later, the cart stops again. The driver steps down. Looks back into the darkness to see if the escorts are still there. But there is no sign of them. Suddenly, the lamp under the cart is blown out by a gust of wind. Just before the light goes out, Giyasji thinks the driver looked vaguely familiar. Then he recognizes him, but cannot believe his eyes. He must be mistaken! Will he dare to call him by his name? 'Let's keep going, son,' he finally says, his voice a desperate plea, 'Only two miles to go now. Until the final talaq. You must hear it spoken. Since the rest seem to have fled. Fled out of fear. Fled out of bearing witness. You will listen. You will be witness. Will the final talaq have one witness, or none at all? I can't seem to tell any more. At least the angels in the sky can testify that my son has laid not a finger on Medina. Not hurt her. You must tell Sukhobas all this. Go to him, tell him Zaheda lives. My daughter is not dead. You'll tell him all this, won't you?'

Then he begins to recite the surah again, faster and faster. Medina bursts into tears. And in the darkness Sukhobas cries out, his voice so strange and twisted and terrible. Such a horrible sound that one cannot truly tell if it is sorrowful or not.

How dark it is, how impossible this darkness.

'Who are you?' asks an astonished Giyasji.

'I *don't know*,' says the driver. Then begins to laugh. Then steps down from the cart and hurtles into the darkness. His laughter gives way to tears. He stands there, asking himself, 'Yes, indeed, who are you?' Then answers, 'I *don't know*.' Then begins to run again, to pant and gasp and heave. To stand still and run again. To question. To answer. Then he runs again. Then he keeps on running. Madman Sukhobas runs on and on, faster and faster, as though into the very heart of that infinite darkness.

Isha moves over and sits in the driver's seat. And at the end of the last two miles, he turns and asks: 'Should I give the last talaq, uncle?'

'No!' replies Giyasji, his voice strong and firm.

The cart rolls on. Medina keeps on sobbing, wretched and alone. And the surah rolls on, like a lament. The cart moves on, through the sea of night. With no place really to go.

Sister

Holding the blue-glass hurricane on her head, Ma went down into the moonlight. Down to where the neem tree was. Then she stopped.

I knew that Ma was sleeping.

'You mother,' Toru-mashi had told me, 'walks in her sleep. Careful, she doesn't go near the Mochadoba swamp.'

The Mochadoba was near our house. Its water was transparent, stained with black. Ma did not know how to swim. Born and raised in swamp-and-river-and-canal country, yet she had never learnt to swim. So she had to be watched over every night.

'Will you get your Ma back if she drowns?' asked Toru-mashi, narrowing her eyes.

That fear kept me awake at night. My brothers and sisters knew, even Baba knew, that it was I who kept watch on Ma. Whenever Ma set out, she had to be brought back. Brought back to the house and laid down on the veranda.

Ma kept walking out. I kept bringing her back. Next morning, she never remembered a thing. Those who walk in their sleep don't know that they do so.

When I would tell Ma what had happened, what she had done at night, she would be very embarrassed. Pretend she did not believe a word of what I said.

Has anyone ever heard of a sleepwalking mother? But that did not make me love Ma any less. Rather, because she was thus, I loved her more. And the fear remained—if Ma fell into the water, she would drown.

My brothers and sisters slept peacefully. How could they? Because they knew that I was watching over Ma. Ma slept beside them on the veranda; only in the height of winter would she sleep inside the house. An open veranda—so one could never tell when she'd step off it and wander away. One could not pull the latch and shut Ma in. A veranda was not a room that you could lock its door.

We were five. Two brothers and three sisters. I was the eldest. Baba was the only earning member. And he had to work very hard to feed so many mouths. A *primary-school master*, and a homoeopathy doctor. Which is why the locals called him *Doctor-Master*.

From dawn till 9.30, Baba met his patients in our small drawing room. Then at 10, after bathing and eating, he set off for school. The school is close by. Seven minutes by cycle. Twelve to fourteen on foot. Baba used to ride very slowly. There were very few in the area as calm and courteous as he. He was a well-known and well-respected man. But not a well-off man. Because the only thing his medical practice earned him was great renown. He charged a negligible fee for both his visits and his medicines. After he came back from school, he could not put away his box of homoeopathy medicines until ten at night. Baba has no medical degree. Only his medical reputation, which is great.

I am the *master's* son. What or which *master's* son? Why, *Doctor-Master's* son. *Doctor* was the introductory adjective for *master*. For the rustics who were wont to use professional identifiers, this double identity was a strange exception. But for this same reason, they also respected him a lot. As a *master* too, Baba was well loved. Honest and hardworking. He never caned his students. His voice was sweet and soft. He wore a Bangla half-sleeved shirt and a dhuti. White. Spotless white. He tucked the edge of his dhuti in one pocket, and wore sandals.

In our family, modesty runs very high. As though it were the lustre of gentility. Yet this world is such an immodest place. Because of that modesty, when he handed over medicines but wasn't paid in turn, Baba would say, 'Give it later.'

Long after the disease was cured, the money was still not paid.

I am so ashamed—my mother is pregnant again. This one, for certain, will also be a girl. Whether the child in the belly will be boy or girl—some women could tell by the features of the pregnancy.

'Your mother will have another girl,' Toru-mashi said, 'Don't be sad.' Then patted me on the head a few times and left.

But I could lift my head no longer.

'Look after her.' Toru-mashi said that too.

Those words startled me.

I could no longer concentrate on my studies. The books lie open on the table, yet my mind wants to fly away.

I can't tell whether Ma heard Toru-mashi's words. Ma is staring at me, refusing to blink. Her eyes full of suspicion and anxiety. And guilt.

I am nineteen. I understand everything. I had to appear for my Class Eleven higher-secondary exams this November. I did not have much time. Under so much pressure, how can one properly prepare for an exam?

'You're not studying.'

'Yes.'

'Really?'

Ma came into my room and stood beside me. I closed my book, got up from chair and put on my Hawaiian shirt.

'Where are you going?' Ma asked.

'Yes.'

'Where?'

As I was leaving the room without another word, Ma said: 'I have something to discuss with you, Shontu. It's a secret.'

Suddenly I got angry with her. Keeping my face low, I said softly, 'Whatever discussion you need to have, why can't you have it with Baba? Why me?'

'I can't with Baba.'

'Why not?'

'You'll know as soon as I tell you. You're the one who has to do the job.'

'Job?'

'Yes, job. You'll have to go to Nabipur, and bring Bishtu-kobiraj to me.'

Taken aback, I turned around and looked into her eyes. Ma was so close to me that I could feel her breath.

'Your father's medicines can't cure me,' Ma said, ' And your father won't let me see another doctor. Your father has taken leave from school next weekend. It's your paternal cousin Naren's sacred-thread ceremony. All of you—but me—will go. I want Bishtu to come on any one of those days and see me somehow. Understand?'

Ma moved away and leant against the wall. Her eyes shone with tears.

I had been a little surprised at first; but was even more astonished by the rest.

'You won't go to the ceremony?'

'How can I? Pennampur is so far away. It is not right that your mother spend a night elsewhere—isn't that so? Your father said that, at your aunt's place, the pond is very deep. The steps down to the water start almost at the door. "Sleepwalking woman! Is there any guarantee you won't cause a disaster at a sacred ceremony! Besides, you should not travel now." I don't want to be a laughing stock either.'

Ma rushed out of the room. I understood some of what she'd said, the rest remained obscure. I sensed that she was trying to hide something. Late in the afternoon, she went to the clay oven in the courtyard and, even though there wasn't much firewood, began preparations for our dinner, .

The oven was an eternal problem. Ma used twigs and branches and dry jute stems as firewood. And this firewood was very hard to find. Scavenging bits and pieces from other people's gardens and orchards was as tedious as it was shameful. A job that was, more often than not, mine.

Whatever little farmland we owned, all of it, thanks to the bhag record, was cultivated according to the sharecropping system. We got barely anything, at most a cart and a half of dry jute stems. Half of which was used to redo the fencing round our courtyard; the other half as firewood. It lasted for about two months.

We were Brahmans. There were only two or three Brahman families in these parts. Not living side by side but spread across the village, in Kolupara, Kamarpara, Palpara and Jugipara. The rest were Muslims. In places such as this, the Brahmans are meant to be especially revered.

I stepped down to the courtyard, the chopper in my hand. I was supposed go to Dhola Qazi's orchard, to collect firewood. The Qazis never stopped us from pulling down the dry branches off their mango trees. Yet, I felt ashamed every time I went.

Standing by the oven, Ma said, 'Does anyone go to other people's gardens in the evening, that too brandishing a chopper? Dhola Qazi came to your father, told us not to. Said, "In town, the Brahmans cook on coal fires. And here you're sending your son to chop branches from other people's trees? It doesn't look good." Your father said, "But this is not the town, Mian—this is a village." '

As soon as Ma finished speaking, Baba walked in, pushing his cycle. From its handles hung his medicine bag and a cloth bag for vegetables.

It was a Saturday. Autumn was here. But the air still reeked of water-rotten jute. Outside the house stood bunches of dry jute stems. Our earnings from the sharecropper—one cart for firewood and half a cart for the fence.

It was a Saturday, so Baba's school had ended at two. Now it was half past four. After school, Baba rode his cycle to the homes of his patients—pretending to check up on them, but in reality collecting fish and vegetables and other such offerings in exchange for the fees he was never paid. Today he'd been to the fishermen's neighbourhood, then ridden on the dirt track along the fields and past the swamp.

'Nibhanoni, put the fish on a plate. It's a kalbosh, weighs three quarters less of a seer. Such a fish is rare in our river. Gokul Malla caught it and had a hard time giving it away. But "Take it—how else do I repay your debt? Just a fish, after all, but still . . ." I cured his daughter's diarrhoea, that too so soon after she'd had her baby. That's why he's so grateful. But you—why are you carrying about that chopper at this hour?'

'How will I light the oven?' Ma said, 'There's not a single bit of firewood.'

'People are stuck with this same problem, Nibhanoni. Now these first fruits, for example, they're meant to be offered to us, the Brahmans. But I had to tear them off, and help myself. I, Balai Mukherjee, don't care whether that Qazi or his kin remembers to offer them to me.' And Baba turned his cloth bag upside down on the veranda.

'What have you done, Baba? You're a thief! You shouldn't have stolen that fruit! Wait, Ma—five fresh cucumbers, don't touch even one. The Muslims offer their first fruit to Khoda at the mosque. These cucumbers will have to go back to Dhola Qazi.'

In shame and despair, I hurled the large chopper to the ground. Ma was stunned, and Baba astonished. Just then, a bird flew up from somewhere and, twitching its long tail, began to hop and skip on our clothesline and then on the edge of our water tub.

Every so often its tail got caught in something and then it ruffled and shuffled to set itself free.

Ma stood near the oven, trembling. Watching the bird struggling to free its tail. Baba's face had clouded over with shame.

But there was something he was trying to say. As soon as I put the cucumbers back in the bag, he asked, 'Then doesn't a Brahman have a right to anything? My forefathers were feudal landowners. Once upon a time, all these acres, all of this 22 mauza, belonged to us. Can such a Brahman be a thief? Even if I am poor, I am still a part of God.'

Suddenly Toru-mashi walked in. At the sight of her, Ma seemed to grow even more fearful. The fish had fallen off the plate and was now jumping about on the veranda, gasping for air. And the bird was calling louder and louder. As though together, bird and fish, were filling the slightly damp, autumn evening air with a message of doom.

I picked up the bag and got off the veranda.

'What's happened?' I asked Toru-mashi.

'Stuck his hand through the fence, and grabbed the cucumbers from Qazi's field—what to say! Mohsin Qazi was behind the scarecrow, he saw it all. He didn't want to embarrass the Brahman, so he didn't step forward. But—of all people—Qazi-saheb asked *me* to come here and see for myself.'

'This is not right, Torulata,' said Baba, gravely, 'What kind of sis-ter-in-law are you! You've come to search your brother-in-law's house on the Qazi's orders? Did I not heal the Qazi's wife enteric? You lot hadn't even heard of the disease! He who saves a life, can he not be a part of God? Which other man is a doctor here? Who else a well-born brahman? Who?'

'Only you, Jamai-babu. But this self-help habit is not good. Your eldest son is an adult now. If you do something bad, he's the one who feels ashamed. Why do you do such things? Why can't you just ask?'

'Are you calling me a thief?' Baba asked, irate.

'Why will I? I am talking about bad habits. Don't you know what you do? Son, let's go, let's give back these new cucumbers. This village is a Muslim village. You are a Brahman—but he too is a Qazi, no less. His drawing room is already full of people. Can't say what judgement they'll pass on you.'

'Is that so?' Baba roared, 'Wait, don't go.' I am taken aback—Baba, so timid and calm, why was he acting like this? If he carried on like this, how could I ever go to Qazi's orchard and collect firewood?

Baba ran across to me and snatched the bag. Stuck his hand into it, brought out the five tender cucumbers and gobbled them up in a flash. All my siblings had come out by then, and were standing around us. Baba ate up the cucumbers so quickly that we just stood there, staring, unable to stop him.

Ma buried her face in her hands and sank to the ground, sobbing in shame.

Then, whimpering in fear, she cried, 'Whenever a girl child comes to my womb, this man acts like this, Toru. You don't know your brother-in-law! How can he eat another man's crop like that? Eat what was owed to Khoda? Do you think they'll let him go? From behind the scarecrow, the Qazi himself saw it all. What do we do now? Oh God, I can walk in my sleep—but I can't run away. Or I would have run away now. Torulata, my sister, save us.'

Dismayed at Ma's words, Toru-mashi dropped to the veranda and then sat there helplessly, her hand against her cheek. The fish jumped once. The long-tailed bird flew away.

Toru-mashi, her hand still against her cheek, watched the fish jump about for a few moments. Then suddenly she grabbed it and began to scale and cut it to pieces. Ma was so astonished that she stopped crying. Baba slunk away into the drawing room. Even at such a moment, there was a patient waiting.

Then the sun set. A fresh round of dry jute stems were burnt in the oven, and that new kind of fish, that rare fish, was cooked. Baba sat down to eat. As if he had no shame whatsoever.

Baba ate alone. We did not touch the fish.

'Don't eat that fish,' Mashi had told us, 'Your father will eat alone.'

It was an emotional game. We never cook a whole meal with jute stalks—the stalks are thin and light, their fire is weak and short-lived; they are kindling at best. Ma used to hoard them all through the year, use only a little every day.

Baba ate his fill and then, burping loudly, said, 'Kalbosh, a rare fruit of the river. And cucumbers, first fruit. You can't keep a good burp down, son. *Gheu!* Can you smell the cucumbers, son? Let the Qazi-kin come, let them shout and beat me—I have nothing to say. But I don't know why, Torulata, I am so drawn to other's things. My stomach hurts, Nibha. I hope I have some medicine for it. *Gheu!* Can you smell it, son? Can you?'

I look up at my father—and see silent tears trickling down his face.

II

This is not Nibhanoni's story nor Balai Mukurjee's nor Tarulata's. This is my story. Or my sister Ekshona's story.

When she came into Ma's womb—that's when the story began.

Later that day, when evening darkened further, Toru-mashi drew me outside. And, walking down the village road, she said, 'We're not going to Qazi, Shontu. What will I tell the Qazi if I go? That brother-in-law has eaten up the cucumbers? Or that he is not a thief? A sleep-walking mother and a kleptomaniac father—you poor boy! Do you think any good will come out of Bishtu-kobiraj? There's no end to his bad name.'

'Why?' I asked, scared.

The village road is much higher than the fields below, on either side. The moon rose with a ripple of light in the enchanting autumn night sky. We came closer to the 12-bigha plot that was Qazi's. There, on bamboo frames, were creepers full of cucumber, ridge gourd, bitter gourd and so much more. Nearby stood the scarecrow.

'What bad name, mashi?'

'Some of the women die during abortion. Who kills them? Bishtu! Yet there is no end to female foeticide. Your mother's planning . . . '

'Enough, mashi. No need to go on.'

Suddenly I froze. Qazi stepped out from behind the scarecrow. Followed by Bishtu Kobiraj.

I began to run.

Dear sister, Ekshona, I could save you. I am sending this letter to your hostel address.

Holding the blue-glass hurricane on her head, our fully pregnant mother Ma walked down into the waters of the Mochadoba. I brought her out. Then she gave birth to you.

'A Black Cloud Gathers . . .'

Father was in the storage business. He stored rice grown in the Rarh. The same district, but the land to the East was Bhorh and to the west was Rarh. And to another side was Kalantar. Such was the triple nature of the soil. Bhorh sloped down to the banks of the Padma while Rarh ground was higher ground, undulating. The rice grew better there. Not so much the fruits and vegetables. In Kalantar, the harvest was most plentiful. The soil there blacker than the blackest of buffaloes. People from Bhorh went to Kalantar to work as seasonal labour. For them, going to Kalantar was as good as going abroad. So, did Kalantar—a different time—signify for them Deshantar—a different homeland? Not only did they travel to the outermost edge of the district, but also some more, a long way off. Did people go willingly all that way? No, they went because they didn't want to starve to death. They used to go, once upon a time. In those days, the land yielded more crops. The Aush in the monsoon, the Amon in late autumn or the Choiti in the spring.

Of course, the storage business has always been a rogue's business. Not fit for a gentleman. Father's temper was as severe as a lord's.

Everyone was afraid of him. Afraid of his expressions when he spoke. With his caterpillar eyebrows, his white-bristle-edged ears, his hairy nostrils—he could not look at anyone without an angry frown.

'Who's this son of a seed-eating, root-gobbling shit? What do you want? Watch out, swine, don't you dare touch my feet!'

'I'm your humble servant, babu. I'm your village kin. I'm Ketan Paramanik. Thrash me with your shoes if you will. My mother and I lived off the seeds. There was a famine—we could save nothing. Please give me another loan, babu, just one more dhama of Betai seed.'

'Man's an orator it seems! Let me remember who's whose kin! Come here—are you brave enough to look at me? Look me in the eye, and ask me once more. Here we're having a drought and he comes wanting seeds.'

'Babu, Seal's half-almanac says the monsoon will come early. There'll be floods. All my neighbours will sow Betai on the bank of the Padma. But I—where will I get the seeds? Where but you?'

'Look at me! First clear the last season's dues, then come to touch my feet. You couldn't grow any rice from the Begunbichi seeds you took last year. First talk of that loan, then we'll see.'

Ketan Paramanik fell silent. He was *half*-goldsmith, *half*-farmer. On his bald head sparkled beads of sweat. What an obvious trap he had fallen into! Not half a goldsmith, more like a quarter. His fingers couldn't do the fine work. So instead of gold, he worked on simpler silver items.

It was not only a storage business. It was a bonded-loan business too. We need to know what and how. And in order to understand the business, we need to first understand what a seed-eater is. A farmer who can't save any seeds for next time, who eats them because he's so poor—such a man is a seed-eater. Seeds are the foundation of a home. No matter how difficult things got, farmers always saved the seeds. That is, they were meant to. Many had no option but to eat them. This seed-eating class was loaned seeds by Baba—he tied them to him with the loan. In Father's hands, the seed-loans were like mortgages. Of course, mortgage here is a minor slip of the tongue for storage.

That seed-eater was the world's worst insult as well as curse was something that Annapurna had understood even as a child.

Even as a child, she could tell Betai seeds from Begunbichi. Betai seeds were black-skinned, fat and thick. Father stored Nona seeds too. One needed to know the difference between Nona and Betai: one did not die in water, for water was its friend. That is, as long as the water was turbulent or excessive. Such was Nona. Under regular conditions, Nona managed to grow well enough in still water.

Betai was different. It had style—Annapurna had seen it for herself. Their Betai seeds used to flourish in the lap of the river. Its head held high, the Betai would stand tall above the waters. When the river waters rose up in flood, that's when Betai showed its true talent—no matter how high the waters rose, Betai rose even higher. The body of the Betai was jointed, like a human's. Knees, waist, chest, neck—it seemed to have lips too. And a suppleness somewhat akin to cane. Thin white roots grew at its joints, in bunches.

Rain above, floodwaters below. Where does Betai go? Its neck goes underwater, then its lips, soon even its forehead. And water-creeper Betai drowns. Stays underwater for two-and-a-half days. Annapurna comes to the flooded river with her father. The stream alongside the river is flooded too. There's water everywhere. Full to the brim. The river's dam had cracked, so all the roads were flooded and everyone was soaking wet as they waded through the floods. If the river comes down by even three inches, if the sky relents a little, then the Betai will rise again, will show its head once more to the sun.

'Dear God, let it be so. Let the river slow down, let the sky grow clear—let them give Betai just one more chance. Hail thee, god of river and water, hail thee, god of sky, save us, save us . . . Rise, Betai, rise, show us your face . . .' Annapurna prayed as hard as she could.

The thought of the Betai underwater hurts Annapurna even today. Her father could sense her anguish. 'Don't be sad, my mother,' he'd say, 'Betai will rise again. This rice-daughter can stay like that for three, even four days. She won't die, just be a bit tired, that's all. She can hold her breath for a long, long time. Though this time it's been two and a half days already. I don't know how she'll live.'

'How will she, Baba?'

'She's the poor farmer's staple. The rice she gives is heavy, thick, coarse. The babus detest it. They prefer *fine* grain. This rice they can't digest.'

'Are you a babu, then, Baba? You don't eat it either.'

'I'm not a babu, Annapurna. I'm a lender.'

'That's bigger than the babus!'

'Yes.'

'Why?'

'Because the babus know only the alphabets. Not seeds.'

'What should I do, Baba?'

'You are Annapurna, goddess of bounty. If the hungry pray for rice, give them rice. If they want seeds, then give them seeds.'

'Nona–Pathorkuchi–Begunbichi–Betai–Bashomoti?'

Her father had burst out laughing. 'No Bhorh farmer sows any Bashomoti. This is rain-and-flood land. So I haven't stored any.'

'Why not?'

'What if the floods devour all the seeds? If the seeds are lost, then I'll be a criminal. Everyone knows I have every kind of seeds, and that I lose none. The seed-eaters remain assured that even if their crop is lost, my stock remains intact. I am Golokpoti the Seed-Keeper, after all. I make sure I get my pound of flesh. You will do so too. Just one anna profit per rupee loan—no more. Per dhama of seed, just one small bowl of seed extra. So if they take a loan of one dhama, they give back one dhama and one bowlful.'

'Do you think I'll be able to?'

'Yes, of course,' Baba said, smiling sweetly at her anxious face.

'But I'm just a girl,' young Annapurna whispered to herself. She knew that girls didn't spend forever in their father's homes. Only God knew to which distant island home her father would marry her off. Whose home would she go to? What kind of man would he be?

There was a young man she liked. Should she tell her father about him? He lived in Akheriganj, where the river was especially terrible, always flooding its banks. The boy had come with a sack, to borrow some Betai seeds. He hadn't looked at all like a farmer's son. More like Lord Krishna, that unknown boy from an unknown land.

'Who are you?' asked Annapurna.

'Indra,' he answered shyly.

'Indra what?'

'We are Ojhas.'

'You know the spells?'

'Spells?'

'Spells that cure snakebite—you know them?'

'No.'

'Then what do you know?'

Indra fell silent. A bit bewildered by her question. His confusion made Annapurna burst into peals of melodious laughter. And he began to look and feel even more foolish.

'My grandfather knew the spell,' he finally managed to stammer, 'Chhoto Chowdhury in Shetherdighi was bitten by a snake. Everybody knows, my grandfather did the spell and brought him back to life. In return, Chhoto Chowdhury donated some land to my grandfather. Most of that spell-land is now eaten away by floods. Whatever remains lies in the river's lap. Father said, "Go, Indranath, go borrow some Betai seeds." Will you give us some? Only half a maund will do.'

'You have no seeds?'

'No.'

'Why not?'

'We have no Betai seeds.'

'Do you have Nona seeds?'

'No.'

'So what do you have?'

'We have nothing.'

'Do you want to buy some seeds?

'No. Don't you give them as loans?'

'Yes, we do.'

'Then give them to me on loan.'

Indranath Ojha went back to Akheriganj with his sack almost full of Betai seeds.

But, by the end of the year, he came back for more. Annapurna realized he and his family were seed-eaters. The thought seemed to crush her a little. 'You won't get any more,' her father said, 'First give back what Annapurna gave you earlier.'

'Babu, the flood swept away everything—what am I to do? It was Betai, yet it rotted away, could not stand above the waters. Please give me a loan for this year—I'll repay both years at once. I swear by Goddess Manasa I'll repay your loan.'

'Oh you oath-taker, promise-maker. Can you drive a cart? I have seven carts leaving for Rarh. Drive one of them to and fro—that's all. That will do. Come back, and I'll give another loan. Go—or forget about it. There'll be no seeds for you. Annapurna, you're not to open the store for him.'

Golokpoti flung his colourful gamchha round his shoulders and strode off to the fields.

Annapurna was standing by the door. Staring thoughtfully at Indranath. Baba had told her not to open the silo for him, the one where the seeds were stored. Which meant that Baba had not believed Indranath entirely.

'I don't know spells,' said a frightened Indranath, with a pleading glance at Annapurna, 'But Father does. He's not a big shaman like grand-father, but he does know the spells. In our village, people respect him a lot. If I lie, Father's spell will fail. My father's spell will be broken.'

'It seems you've learnt your letters.'

'Yes, but they're no good to me. Why—why do you ask?'

'Just curious. Do you believe in the spells?'

'I don't. But my father does. Don't you?'

'No.'

'Oh!' Indra lowers his frightened eyes. Then, shoulders drooping, he turns and begins to walk away, the empty sack still folded under his arm.

All the way home, a downcast Indra thought of many things. What the spells accomplished he had no idea. His forefathers, his father, they had all lived by the spells. The spells were very real for them. The spells had got them land. Though an ojha can never ask for something in return. His faith prevented him from selling the spells. Bring down the poison and give back life—but take nothing in exchange. Chhoto Chowdhury's donation of property could not in truth be called an exchange; the land has not been asked for, after all. The life-restoring spell, it spread nectar through a man. And the joy of restoring life—that was the supreme joy. To possess the power of such spells unleashed such extreme desires in man. Neither father nor grandfather put much effort into the land. That spell-land was now in the river's path. Father looked at it scornfully a few times, and carried on going from village to village, casting spells. He was an incredible ojha. Lived in a house but no householder was he.

Hence Indra, despite being admitted to *college*, had to abandon his dreams of earning an education. Had to, instead, tend to home and hearth. He was suspicious of the spells. But he'd never uttered a mean word to the spell-maker. His father was bringing strangers back to life, and here, back home, mother and son were starving to death! Even then, in their eyes, the father was an other-worldly being. Otherworldly and deserving of respect.

Last year, when Indra had come to borrow seeds, he had spoken to Annapurna about the spells but not about his father. He prefers to conceal from others all talk of his miraculous parent. Because it was his spells that were killing them now.

Indra walked on, his head low. The road entered a field, curved in a half circle and then carried on. Not field so much as farmland as far as the eye could see. They were Ojhas. Low castes. And he hadn't even learnt the spells. Golokpati Chakraborty had refused him a loan. What a terribly hard man he was! Those bristly ears, those caterpillar eyebrows, those hairy nostrils—what a cruel visage it all added up to! He had made fun of Indra. Rejected his pleas. Are all seed-keepers as whimsical as the gods? How could a man like this have gathered a silo full of seeds?

It was Chaitra. The seed-keeper's fields were aglow with the beautiful colour of the sweet pumpkin crop. Sweet pumpkins that were being piled up in seven bullock carts. To take them to Rarh. The pumpkins would be exchanged for sacks full of rice. Indra saw: seven carts, but six drivers. That was why the seed-keeper had given him the task.

'You, you there, are you coming with us? We're one driver short. Bongshi's down with dysentery. Betai does that to you, sets your tummy rumbling. Heavy rice, after all. Since master's told you to do it—it's not that you won't be paid. Besides, you're a seed-eater. So better do as master says. Let's go to Rarh. We'll take the shortest route—go and come fast enough.'

The head driver was very persuasive. 'I don't have any clothes for the ride,' Indra said. 'It's quite a long way off.'

'OK. We'll get you some. Some *readymades*. Shop's at Ullashpur crossing. Can we do that, babu?'

Golokpati nods, gives permission. Says: 'Make sure you give him a cart with a good pair of bullocks. And whatever else, clothes and things . . . The manager will give you the money.'

Indra was given the cart with the strongest, most well-behaved bullocks. His cart was second in line. Indra thought: in the end, I've become a cart driver. Ferrying pumpkins to Rarh. What an amazing turn of events. But he was even more amazed when they stopped at Ullashpur crossing and he was bought new clothes. As soon as he entered the shop, he saw Annapurna sitting on the floor. She was the one, the seed-keeper's daughter, who chose what he would wear.

'Since you're the one doing the choosing,' the head-driver exclaimed, 'he can be rest assured of quality. Hey Indranath, come here. But, my mother, don't choose things too *fine*. Or the Ojha's son will be embarassed.'

'Why will he? He'll have to wear whatever I give him. He's not a cart-driver like you lot. He's going along only because he wants to,' said she and, picking up an expensive shirt, glanced up at Indra with her beautiful eyes.

'Why would I want to go? I'm going because I *have* to. I've never worn such expensive clothes. Please, not these.'

'Why not? Not even if I give them to you?'

'No, not that. Actually, they don't suit me. We have eaten up your seeds, Annapurna. If I strut about in clothes like this, I'll feel like a shameless fool. You won't understand.'

These words struck Annapurna like a blow. 'We have eaten up your seeds, Annapurna'—this incredibly pitiful statement seemed to coil and twist within her. Never had her heart behaved this way before. She gave a little shiver. She had never met a seed-eater like this. Shy, courteous, such a tender-hearted young man. What was he so ashamed of? Those whose hunger makes them eat seeds—do they have any shame left?

'I won't understand,' says Annapurna softly to herself. Then, throwing the shirt at Indra, she says, 'You will wear whatever I give you. No one talks back to us. Here, take this dhuti as well. And shoes? Don't you have shoes? Listen, Kinkor-da, buy him some shoes, from Sen's shop. Baba has an account there. They'll make a note of it. Now, go.'

Then the carts came back with rice. Exactly seven days later. In his new clothes and shoes, Indra looked like a gentleman, like a son-in-law come visiting. Golokpati was quite astonished at the sight. He couldn't even recognize him at first.

'Kinkor,' he asked, his voice crackling with contempt, 'who's this?'

'Your cart-driver, master,' Kinkor replied fearfully.

At one end of the long veranda stood Annapurna, near the door. She too had been startled by her father's tone. 'My driver, and dressed like this! Who gave him these clothes? Driver or dandy—who do you think you are?'

'I am Indra. Indranath Ojha. From Akheriganj village. And in your debt.'

'Then why the hell are you wearing these clothes?'

'I did not want them, babu.'

'Then why have you worn them? And not yet cleared your debt from last year!'

'No, babu.'

'So then tell me, my dandy darling, do you feel no shame? Do you know what you look like?'

Suddenly, at these words, the heart of this seed-filled universe began to tremble and slowly disappear into a hitherto-unknown darkness. Indra felt as if he was falling into a bottomless pit. The world began to taste of Betai. Heavy, thick and coarse.

'You've eaten off me. And now you're out to ruin me. Take off those clothes. And bring that sack of yours. Hey, who's there? Give him some seed.' With that, Golokpoti walked off into the house.

Indra's head was pounding. He felt dizzy. And his throat had run dry. His veins throbbed so hard he felt they would burst. He didn't know what to do. What *did* he look like? These lovely clothes, he'd put them on only a krosh or so ago. As soon as he had stepped out of the shop, as soon as he was out of Annapurna's sight, he had taken them off and put on his old torn clothes. He had been too embarrassed to wear those beautiful things for the rest of the ride. Even on the way back, he hadn't wanted to put on the shirt and shoes and dhuti from Annapurna. The other drivers were the ones who had insisted, who had teased him. Which is why, even more, he hadn't wanted to touch them.

What *did* he look like? Like a dandy? All the way to and fro, the drivers had teased him, called him 'son-in-law'. Sometimes in the villages, some young men would be nicknamed this way. So much so that everyone tended to forget their real names.

Indra hadn't had a chance to look in a mirror. To see himself dressed up in a seed-keeper's clothes. There had been no stretch of water to look into, either. Nor someone else's eyes.

Indra was ashamed. To have come running to Madhupur all the way from the Padma land of Akherigunj, to beg for Betai seeds. For Betai was not to be had everywhere. Those who did have them, they kept aside enough for farming and ate the rest. Golokpati had a good reputation. He never turned away anyone without a fistful of seed. Perhaps even God borrowed seeds from him. Should God ever run out a particular seed, it was Golokpati to whom he would come to for a loan.

Golokpati has a thousand and one seed pots. Those pots were stored in a huge earthen room. On every pot was written in chalk the name of the seed, written by the seed-keeper's daughter. She had enough education to spell each one correctly. Indra suddenly wanted to walk through that room. Seeds, only seeds, seeds everywhere. Oh God, the great seeds you scattered once now lie here in supreme slumber.

Indra could write on a grain of rice. Six carts of rice waited outside Golokpati's house. One cart was full of Bashomoti. The one driven by Indranath. How amazingly fragrant that rice was! One of the sacks had a tiny hole. A few grains trickled out of it into Indra's palm. One night, in Kandi, while the drivers rested beneath a tree, Indra went to a shop nearby and bought a fine, gold-tipped needle. Made a brush out of it and began to trace letters on the grains: 'Bashomoti, you are mine.' Nineteen letters on nineteen grains. Then he tied the grains up in a small piece of cloth. Nineteen letters. Nineteen grains.

This was another magic. Singing a line from the snakebite spell, he blew once on the grain bundle now held tightly in his fist. 'On the shores of Kalidaha, a beautiful black cloud gathers.' Such went the line. As good as a snakebite spell. The beautiful black cloud was in fact Krishna. As though Indra were casting a spell. On whom? But Indra wasn't as foolish as that! He'd never utter a name and risk death! Merely raise his fist. And say: This bundle holds rice. Rice. She who's named after rice, I cast a spell on her.

Indra took off his new shirt. Blew the rice dust off the ground. Fetched his gamchha from the cart, wiped a part of the floor clean and carefully placed his new shirt and dhuti there. Took off his new shoes and set them down by a pillar on the veranda. Put on his own shirt and pyjamas. His own torn rubber slippers held together with a safety pin. One of the soles was worn so thin, he feared for the moment when it would fall off. Indra was always fearful. So he walks carefully. And worries all the time about the safety pin slipping off.

Those are the slippers that Indra now wore with care. He had washed his dirty shirt in Rarh, with Lifebuoy soap. That too had grown thin with use, a bit of its collar had torn. That same shirt he now wore with care. Tied the clean but crumpled pyjama strings firmly round his waist.

Then, his eyes full of apprehension, he looked up to where Annapurna was standing by the door and said, 'Give me my sack.' And saw, at that same moment, how her eyes were shining with tears.

Indra's words seem to startle Annapurna. At a loss about what to do now, she walked across the veranda, picked up the sack and gave it back to him.

'You won't take some, then?'

'Take what?'

'Betai seeds?'

'Give me some, then,' Indra placed the sack at Annapurna's feet, its mouth open. Annapurna brought out the scales and bowls and measured out the seeds. Half a maund. Then, when she was done, she tied the mouth of the sack with string. Her fingers touched Indra's. And a tremor ran through her. She lowered her eyes.

Then, suddenly, she looked up and said in sharp seed-keeper tones: 'Now, you owe me one maund and two bowls. Once the rice grows, you can pay me back.' That behind her words lay a deep hurt— Indranath could not tell.

Indra left the sack where it was and turned to leave. He could not bear to meet the eyes of his seed-keeper. With one leap, he was down on the stairs. Then, head hanging low, he walked across the courtyard, out towards the road.

'Won't you take the seeds?' Annapurna called out.

Indra did not respond.

'Won't you take the seeds?' Annapurna's words were now a plea.

'No.'

'Please take them, Indra. Please, don't be angry. Please, listen. Don't go. Baba says, no one should go back empty-handed.'

Indra stopped. Turned around. 'I'm an Akheriganj man, Annapurna. Akheri means the end. Nothing lies beyond. Beyond, there's only water. No earth. No country. We never get angry with anyone. I know we can never pay back your loan. I think now, though, it's better to die than to live as a seed-eater. The Padma's rushing at me, Annapurna. I don't have much time. Goodbye.'

Then, walking back a part of the way, he drew close to the cowshed. In a corner of its low-hanging roof, he tucked away the little grain-and-cloth bundle. Then began to run across the courtyard, out to the road.

Annapurna rushed to the cowshed. Pulled out the bundle. Untied it and found the nineteen grains. And was astonished. This was not something she could understand. She tied up the bundle again. Then ran out onto the road. Indranath was speeding away, rushing off somewhere into the horizon. Annapurna stood there, frozen, tears welling up her in eyes.

The tiny rice bundle in her hand—she didn't throw it away. Yet all evening she couldn't quite figure out what to do with it. Evening lengthened into night. The Chaitra wind rose and fell in waves on the terrace of their cemented house. A strange dust seemed to obscure the moon. As she stared up at it, it struck her that the bundle might be part of a spell. Why else would Indra put it there so furtively and rush off without a word?

She found the whole thing quite amusing. Whom had poor Indra cast a spell on? On Annapurna? So that she became his? Tormented by such thoughts, her eyes grew moist again. She went downstairs, poured herself a glass of water, then climbed up to the terrace again. But she still could not read the nineteen letters traced by Indra on the nineteen grains. That he had traced them at all was beyond her wildest imaginings. Suddenly, she put them in her mouth and washed them down with water. And at once began to feel a strange heaviness descend upon her limbs. She wanted to laugh. And to cry.

Annapurna could not sleep that night. Tossed and turned in bed. At the crack of dawn, it occurred to her that Indra did not know any spells. Then why he did hide that bundle? He knew no spells, true, but he knew someone who did. One of them might have done the spell for him. The more she thinks about things, the more Annapurna feels she has fallen in love. Her heart seems to have grown amazingly restless.

'Indra has cast a spell on me,' she whispered. 'So I will have to go.'

'Where will you go?' the bright red rooster atop the cowshed asked. This wicked bird ate up all the seed, flew into the store as soon as the door swung open. No one could keep it at bay. Its feet were incredibly strong, its wings lined with incredible courage. Its claws razor sharp. Its voice exulting with seed-eating joy. Its name was Chunilal.

'To he who's not as brave as you,' replied Annapurna.

'To whom?' asked the rooster, blinking its eyes, 'To whom?'

'To he who doesn't have wings as cunning as you. To him.'

'And who is that?'

'To he who doesn't have your claws, your beak. To him I'll go. Go for ever.'

'Take seeds with you. Betai seeds. It's a two-and-half-day journey.'

'Of course. I'll take seeds of every kind. Whatever seeds it takes to build a home, I will take with me. I'll go—and I'll not come back, Chunilal.'

'You're the daughter of a Brahman seed-keeper! And you leave us for Kalidaha? Will the world let you go?'

'Be quiet. I've told you already, I'm not coming back.'

Annapurna sent for the driver and began to prepare the cart. As she filled it with her things, she saw in her mind's eye, somewhere, some other sky, slowly adorned with a line of blue-black clouds. So too would she adorn her husband, her Indranath. 'On the shores of Kalidaha, a beautiful black cloud gathers.'

In Annapurna's hands, it seemed as if all the world's seeds gathered and grew more beautiful. Apart from rice, she took seeds for ridged gourd, chilli, bitter gourd, cucumber, pumpkin, melon, brinjal and snake gourd—whatever was necessary. She took seeds for mustard, gram, wheat, barley, linseed and sesame. Everything that could grow and flourish in Bhorh soil. It seems the seeds were bedecked with crowns today as they set off with her, with their Annapurna.

Annapurna's bullock cart reached Akheriganj just before sunset. This was where India was almost at an end. The Padma here was roaring, deaf to all cries, blind to all devastation and stubborn. The hundred-thousand-million tongues of Padma licked at home and land like a *villain*. Licked and swallowed whole.

Haranath Ojha, Indra's father, grew fearful at the sight of the seed-keeper's daughter. He grew even more afraid when she stooped to touch his feet. The four mud walls of his little hut and its thatched roof were shaking and rattling, beaten mercilessly by the Padma's fierce and ferocious winds. As though it would fall any minute now.

The driver moved to the cart to start unpacking the seeds. 'I've brought the Betai seeds, father,' Annapurna said, 'Please call your son.'

Haranath stood there, incredulous. He could not utter a word. Then, suddenly, a word stuck deep in his throat seemed to burst forth: 'No.' And he raised his hand at the driver, gesturing him to stop.

'Why not, father? I have come to stay for ever,' said Annapurna. Then spotted, in the distance, Indranath coming back from the river. Bare-bodied. Splashed with mud. Wearing a dirty lungi. And a farmer's wicker hat.

Indranath was astounded. He saw Annapurna's eyes glittering with tears. Then he saw the cart full of sacks. He opened them one by one, dipped his hands into the seeds and examined them carefully. It took him quite a while to go through them all. Then he looked up at her.

'Won't you take them?'

'No.'

'Not a single seed is rotten. I'm giving them to you Indra—won't you take them? Each seed will sprout. Betai will grow, look up at the sun. I'm not going back. I'm never going back. You take them.'

'Not all seeds get soil, my mother,' said Haranath. 'Some fly, some float through the air, through the darkness. In Kalidaha, all lies bare. No clothes. No soul. No heart. So what good will seeds do us, my mother? For as long as this spell-land is not swallowed by the Padma, that's how long we seed-eaters have gone to you, begging for seeds. If we have no land, what will we do with seeds? Yesterday, early in the morning, we lost our land. Now we're moving to Kalantar. You go back now, my mother. Indra, why don't you help tie the bullocks back to the cart.'

'Here, you,' called Indra to the driver, 'come give me a hand.'

How hard seemed Indra's face. His arms.

'It's dark now, didi,' said the driver, 'best sit inside, beneath the shade. Come.'

Wiping her eyes with the edge of her saree, Annapurna climbed into the cart. Sat there, looking at all of them.

'Won't you come a part of the way, Indra?' she suddenly called out, 'At least until the main road?'

Indra began to walk behind the cart. 'We're not the only ones who've lost, Annapurna,' he said suddenly, 'The Padma breaks everything every year. Neighbourhoods, markets, shops and stores. Everything. Once in a while, they write about it in the papers.'

'Why did you come away that day without the seeds I gave you?'

'I came home and found our seed-land drowned in the river. There's nothing to worry about any more. Everything is now as clear as water.'

'Why did you cast a spell on me, Indra?'

'Spell?'

'Yes. Nineteen grains. I counted. Tell me, what made you feel so brave?'

'Those are just some letters I'd written on rice. Why would I cast a spell? I don't believe in spells.'

'What did you write?'

'Why should I tell you?'

'You might as well. I'm going back anyway.'

'Bashomoti, whose are you?'

'That's twenty!'

'I'm not brave enough for any less. Thank God the land is gone. Or how would you have gone back home, Annapurna?'

On the way home, each of the nineteen letters came back to Annapurna. Every grain. Every speck. She found each one again in each corner of her mind. Screaming and shrieking and slashing with his claws, Chunilal ripped her heart to shreds. And greedily stretched his beak towards the grains.

'Bashomoti, whose are you?'

'Bashomoti, you are mine.'

Translator's Notes

Italicized words in the translation indicate their use in English in the original Bengali texts.

'Ruku Dewan'

PAGE 1 | 'Nothing but roja-namaz-fitra-jamat-Muharram-akikah . . . to live for.'—A summary of the life of a pious Muslim, strictly adhering to the tenets of Islamic scripture in every aspect, from prayers to food to festivals, from weddings to deaths.

PAGE 2 | 'kalma'—The kalmas or kalimas are the six selected verses from the Qur'an which the Muslims incorporate in their lives as basic moral principles. They are tayyab (purity), shahadat (martyrdom), tamjeed (glorification of Allah), tauhid (oneness of divinity), astaghafar (penitence) and radde kufr (rejecting disbelief).

PAGE 2 | 'qurbani meat and rice'—The ritual slaughter of animals that Muslims perform to symbolically emulate Prophet Ibrahim's willingness to sacrifice his son Ismail to Allah's command.

PAGE 2 | Sonagachhi—Major red-light quarter in Kolkata.

PAGE 2 | Kaloshona—Literally, black-gold, hints at the woman's dark complexion, and shona, an indigenous endearment.

PAGE 4 | 'Maghrib comes and goes on horseback.'—Maghrib is one of the five daily prayers of Islam. Though there are other scriptural interpretations, according to the popular sayings, as Maghrib prayer is scheduled between sunset and nightfall, the time for prayer is very short. This fleeting nature is imagined as Maghrib speeding in and out on horseback.

PAGE 5 | 'ab-e-zamzam'—The water of the zamzam well, located within the Masjid al-Haram in Mecca. Miraculously generated by Allah, and gushing forth thousands of years ago when Ibrahim's son Ismail was left with his mother Hajar in the desert, thirsty and crying. Prophet Muhammad was transported from Masjid al-Haram to Masjid al-Aqsa on the night of Revelation. It is one of the hajj sites for the Muslims.

'Kafan-nama'

PAGE 10 | 'bishahari ojha'—Ojha is a particular caste of people who are believed to have miraculous healing powers to draw out poisons with natural elements and magic chants.

PAGE 10 | 'Madhubas of Madhukhali—what a bitter name!'—That the Sundarbans is a major source of honey in Bengal is reflected in various names of places like Madhukhali. When a child is named Madhu like Madhubas, it signifies the honeyed affection of the parents. Here Madhubas' life becomes a complete antithesis of the honeyed connotation, reflected in the narrator's ironic use of bitter.

PAGE 11 | 'suleymani baidya'—A traditional healer who prescribes semi-precious stones set in rings, bracelets and pendants as cures. In southern Bengal, he often relies more on spells and charms, herbs and powders.

PAGE 12 | 'When Dakshin Rai, the tiger man, strikes . . .'—Bonbibi, the divine power sent by Allah to protect those who enter the forest, is worshipped by all in the Sundarbans. Honey-collectors and wood-cutters offer special prayers to Bonbibi before entering the forest. Bonbibi protects everyone from Dakshin Rai (literally, the lord of the south), the revered deity who rules over the beasts and demons of the Sundarbans. An arch-enemy of Bonbibi, he appears in the guise of a tiger and attacks humans.

PAGE 13 | maktab—'School' in Arabic. An institution providing Islamic scriptural training.

'The Open-Winged Scorpion'

PAGE 21 | 'Uttam Kumar'—One of the most loved and charismatic of Bengali actors (1926–1980).

PAGE 21 | 'Faraizi pattern'—Faraizi, an Islamic reformist movement active in Bengal since the 1830s, instrumental in inculcating the scriptural way of life and thought among the Bengali-speaking Muslims.

PAGE 21 | 'good name'—In many parts of India, a child gets two names: a formal one ('bhalo naam', literally 'good name') for the public space and an informal one ('daak naam' or a name for calling, a pet name) for the intimate, family space.

PAGE 22 | 'MLA *quota*'—Members of Legislative Assembly offer special benefits to their followers to enjoy, in turn, the almost feudal loyalty such largesse usually inspires. Here, the narrator mentions the ruling party's agenda to hegemonize the education sector by appointing its party members to all the significant posts. It does not relate to any constitutional policy of affirmative action for the backward classes.

PAGE 22 | 'Jama'at'—In Arabic, 'jamiat' means 'gathering'. Jamiat Ulema-e-Hind (Council of Indian Muslim theologians), one of the leading organizations of Islamic scholars belonging to the Deobandi school of thought in India, was founded in 1919 by a group of Deobandi scholars. The Jamiat was an active participant in the Khilafat Movement (1919–24) in collaboration with the Indian National Congress and opposed the Partition of India. A faction in 1945 demanded the creation of Pakistan, and came to be known as Jamiat Ulema-e-Islam; currently, it is a political party active in Pakistan. In this story, the author is referring to a socioreligious body, active in spreading the scriptural truths of Islam in different parts of Bengal. Whether such activities have a political base is yet to be ascertained, says Bashar.

PAGE 24 | 'the League candidate could not recover even his deposit!'—A candidate fighting an election has to deposit a sum of money as security. If the candidate does not get one-sixth of the total number of valid votes polled, he or she forfeits the deposit, which is said to be a matter of great shame.

PAGE 24 | 'as though Sakuntala's journey to *her* husband'—Referring to the episode in the Mahabharata later famously adapted into a play by Kalidasa. In it, Sakuntala is separated for a long time from her husband Dushyanta, until a fisherman finds their lost wedding ring in the stomach of a fish. Without the ring, thanks to a curse from an irate sage,

Dushyanta would not be able to recognize her—the sage's curse had wiped his memory clean of Sakuntala.

PAGE 25 | 'bigha'—A traditional unit of land measurement, commonly used in India, though its exact measure may vary from state to state.

PAGE 25 | 'mauza'—A type of administrative district, corresponding to a specific land area within which there may be one or more settlements.

PAGE 25 | 'bahurupi'—Literally, 'a person who has many (bahu) forms (rupa)'. Using a combination of make-up, body paint, masks, costumes, prosthetics, wigs and jewellery, they dress up as religious and/or mythological characters, and go from place to place, performing for money or alms. (See https://www.sahapedia.org/shapeshifters-bediya-bahurupis-birbhum)

PAGE 26 | 'its two extra Chamunda arms'—Chamunda is the fearsome form of Chandi who appeared in the Puranas as Parvati's alter ego. In the Shakta tantric texts, she is one of the 64 Yoginis who roam the cremation grounds and are appeased with animal sacrifice and offerings of wine. In her iconography, she is depicted as sitting on a corpse, meditating and drinking wine from a human skull,

PAGE 27 | 'Her *snow* on my face'—As the cold creams and/or vanishing creams resembled the snow, there was an abundance of this word in the names of the cold creams available in the market. Gradually, snow became a generic name to signify vanishing or cold creams for all brands.

PAGE 27 | 'Protector of the Skies'—In the original, 'Ashmaner daroga'. Ashman (sky) and daroga (police-chief), both Persian loan words in Bangla, are used here as a unique devotional rhetoric to signify the Prophet who is called the guard of the skies,

PAGE 28 | 'Nyada insect'—Type of locusts that infest paddy fields.

PAGE 28 | 'Khoda-Halshahana'—Allah. 'Hal-shahana', in Persian, refers to the majestic stature of Allah.

PAGE 28 | 'Playing *forward*'—In football vocabulary, an attacking game.

PAGE 28 | 'Used to be CP in college'—Chhatra Parishad, popularly known as 'CP', is the student wing of the Indian National Congress in West Bengal. History has seen major campus clashes between the Leftist students' union and CP in the 1980s and 90s.

PAGE 28 | 'Chambal'—Chambal valley in Madhya Pradesh, a state in central-north India, notorious for its dacoits.

PAGE 28 | 'Jiziya'—A tax paid by non-Muslims residing in Islamic lands. Jiziya was introduced in parts of India under the Sultanate in the eleventh century. Its abolition by Mughal emperor Akbar and its re-introduction by Aurangzeb unleashed different dynamics between Muslim and non-Muslim subjects in the Mughal empire.

PAGE 28 | 'And now a new party . . . Faw-Baw-Cong'—Forward Bloc was a coalition partner of the Left Front government in Bengal till 2011. Bashar, in this story, writes specifically about Murshidabad that remained a Congress stronghold in those years. The alliance Bashar refers to between the Forward Bloc (Faw-Baw) and the Congress (Cong) was an entirely local, informal grassroots alliance that did not have any connection with either's official party line.

PAGE 29 | 'Bhikupada Gunahgar'—The surname means 'a sinner' (gunah means sin) in the Islamic scriptural traditions which started to designate the criminal in modern legal rhetoric.

PAGE 29 | '420 cavalry'—Section 420 of the Indian Penal Code refers to 'Cheating and dishonestly inducing delivery of property.' In India, '420' is thus loosely used to refer to good-for-nothings—thieves, smugglers, pickpockets and other petty criminals.

PAGE 30 | 'Tool-man'—Indicating his demotion, hence his fall from a chair/being a chair-man to a tool—or being a stool man.

PAGE 30 | 'Ata was an Eight-*pass*'—He had studied up to, and cleared, Class Eight in school.

PAGE 30 | 'these are the evil Dajjals . . . He will have *kaf-fereth* written on his forehead'—In Islamic eschatological traditions, al-Dajjal is the false messianic figure who appears before the end of time, emerging as an uncontrollable storm that sweeps up everything and then crushes it all. There are various interpretations and descriptions of the impact. First appearing as the Antichrist in pseudo-apocalyptic Christian literature, the idea was reworked in Sunni *hadis* literature and Shia discourses. Dajjal has an ugly and fearful appearance with one blind eye protruding like a floating grape and k-f-r (non-believer, infidel) written on his forehead. Among other interpretations, in the Sunni tradition

Dajjal will be killed after his reign of 40 days or 40 years by Christ, while the Shias aver that Dajjal will be killed by their last imam, Mahdi.

PAGE 30 | Sarat Chandra—Sarat Chandra Chatterjee/Chattopadhyay (1876–1938), renowned Bengali novelist and short-story writer.

PAGE 31 | 'double police station'—Two police stations located so close to each other that areas under their jurisdiction overlap.

PAGE 31 | 'His title will be *Home Guard*'—A special volunteer task force that helps the police.

PAGE 31 | 'BDO'—Block Development Officer. A jest at the expense of the one-eyed assistant who clearly did not have the educational qualifications to rise to this fairly high administrative post.

PAGE 32 | 'the *dry dole* list'—Rations handed out by the government, and usually comprising a combination of rice, wheat and pulses.

PAGE 32 | 'You are an LC member'—Local Committee member of the Communist Party of India (Marxist).

PAGE 32 | 'they are *general body* members'—Of the Communist Party of India (Marxist). Hence, later the hammer and sickle and star above the Biswas doorway.

PAGE 35 | 'tasbih'—A string of rosary made of wooden or plastic beads to keep counting Allah's name.

PAGE 35 | 'Sakina'—Daughter of Husayn, Prophet Muhammad's grandson.

PAGE 36 | 'Buraq'—In the Islamic tradition, Buraq, a celestial creature—a white and winged half-mule, half-donkey—transported Muhammad from Mecca to Jerusalem on the night of Revelation and in his journey through Heaven. Buraq, literally 'lightning' or 'bright', is believed to be the transport for many Abrahamic prophets.

'The Other Quilt'

PAGE 45 | 'A Muslim's wife doesn't prance about, playing Radhika'—Here, the married Tanu's emotions for Ruhul are reprimanded by drawing upon the allusion of the married Radhika or Radha's love for Krishna. This adulterous bonding between Krishna and Radha is the core spiritual metaphor of Vaishnava theology and popular devotionalism.

PAGE 53 | 'firqa'—According to Islamic scholars, there are 73 sects, or firqa, in Islam.

PAGE 54 | 'There is the Surah Nahl in the Qur'an'—In the 68th ayah (verse) of Surah an-Nahl, the sixteenth chapter of the Qur'an containing 128 verses, Muhammad is narrated as bringing Revelation from Allah to the bees'. Nahl literally means 'bees' and Surah Nahl contains a comparison of the industry and adaptability of honey bees with the industry of man. When Ruhul sings about the bees, he simply celebrates and venerates Muhammad.

PAGE 57 | 'Lalon said'—Also known as Fakir Lalon Shah, Lalon Shah, Lalon Fakir (1774–1890). A scholar of Islamic mysticism who blended Tantric, Vaishnavite and Natha yogic theologies with scriptural Sufism in his songs that are popular in Bengal even today. In modern Bangladesh, he has been reclaimed as a reformist figure, as one who preached a syncretic idea of religion and humanism though his spiritual verses.

PAGE 60 | 'Prakriti'—In the philosophical discourses of Samkhya and Yoga, Prakriti, the feminine principle, is the complementary opposite of Purusha, the male principle. The cosmic union of Purusha—the principle of pure consciousness and mobility—and Prakriti—the principle of matter and stasis—is exemplified in the symbol of sexual union in tantric philosophy. Tantrism believes in the ultimate union of consciousness and matter. In this story, the names of the protagonists—Ruhul (Ruh, Arabic for 'the abstract consciousness') and Tanu (Sanskrit loan word, literally, 'the physical body') adds another interpretive layer by hinting at the esoteric theories of the baul based on the Purusha–Prakriti principles.

PAGE 62 | 'Surah Baqara'—Referring to al-Baqara ('The Heifer' or 'The Cow'), the second and longest chapter of the Qur'an, encompassing a variety of topics and containing several instructions, especially about the fast to be kept during the month of Ramzan.

'Night Kohl'

PAGE 68 | 'Bholey-baba paar karega'—Ritual chant, referring to Shiva's endearing name popular in many parts of India, including Bengal, for his bhola (innocent or unworldly) nature. Pilgrims who annually walk from all over Bengal to the popular Shaivite site of Tarakeswar chant this refrain that means Shiva will help them cross the journey, literal or spiritual.

PAGE 69 | 'mouri'—Fennel seeds, often eaten after meals as a digestive and mouth freshener.

PAGE 70 | 'Matric'—The Matriculation examination.

PAGE 72 | 'tiki-poiteys'—Both signs of an upper-caste Hindu. The tiki is the little tuft of hair at the back of an otherwise bald head of a Hindu brahman; the poitey is the brahman's sacred thread.

PAGE 75 | 'khatib'—The person who delivers the sermon (khutbah, literally, 'narration') during the Friday prayer and Eid prayers.

PAGE 79 | 'they transform Ratnakar into Valmiki'—The notorious dacoit Ratnakar, confronted with the pain of a bird-couple pierced with his arrows, expressed his remorse in beautiful poetic language. Then, abandoning his aggression, he turned into renowned Sanskrit poet Valmiki, and recited/composed the Ramayana.

'The Road'

PAGE 86 | 'Asgar'—Asgar was the infant son of Husayn who was martyred in the Battle of Karbala. When Husayn took him to the banks of Euphrates for a drink of water, an arrow, meant for Husayn, pierced the baby Asgar instead.

In the Jari song that follows, the reference is probably to an older son of Husayn named Ali Akbar which, through oral slippage, has become Asgar as well.

PAGE 86 |'Jarigan'—From the Persian Jari/zari for lamentation (hence, song of sorrow) is one of the few indigenous music performances of Bangladesh, West Bengal, Barak and Brahmaputra Valleys. Though varied and divergent in form, most are based on legends about Hasan and Husayn, grandsons of Muhammad and other members of his family at the Battle of Karbala. (See https://www.sahapedia.org/jarigaan)

'The Measure of Land'

PAGE **107** | 'katha'—A traditional unit of land measurement, commonly used in India. In West Bengal, equivalent to 720 square feet.

PAGE **109** | 'maund'—The anglicized name for a traditional unit of mass used in British India, from the mann or mun used in the Mughal Empire.

PAGE **109** | 'ser'—Bengali pronunciation of seer, a traditional unit of weight used across India and equal to 1.25 kg.

PAGE **109** | 'Bashomoti'—Bengali version of Basmati, a variety of long, slender-grained aromatic rice, many varieties of which are traditionally grown in India.

PAGE **109** | 'ryot'—A tenant-cultivator.

PAGE **110** | 'Bargapatta'—Operation Barga (1978–mid-80s) was a land-reform movement in rural West Bengal which aimed to record the names of sharecroppers or 'bargadars'. It also sought to bestow on them legal protection against eviction by their landlords, and entitled them to the due share of the produce.

PAGE **113** | 'Sunnahti beard'—The Sunnah/Sunna is the way of life pre-scribed as normative for Muslims on the basis of the teachings and practices of Muhammad and interpretations of the Qur'an. Muslims consider their beards sacred for they are grown and maintained follow-ing the example set by the Prophet.

PAGE **117** | 'land is over the *ceiling*'—A reference to the Land Ceiling Act, another part of the land-reform movement, which put a ceiling on landholdings in order to redistribute surplus land to the landless.

'Simar'

PAGE **126** | 'FM-passed Quddus'—Fadilul Ma'rif, a three-year Islami theological degree course equivalent to a bachelor's degree in general education.

PAGE **129** | 'as beautiful as a kolabou'—Kolabou is said to be the newly wed bride of the Hindu deity Ganesha in Bengal, A plantain (kola) tree is cut and given a ceremonial bath and then wrapped up in a red-bordered white sari like a wife (bou) as a part of the veneration of Goddess Durga and her family.

'Sister'

PAGE **157** | 'thanks to the bhag *record*'—The government records determining the division and redistribution of land according the Land Ceiling Act. Bhag is literally 'to divide/apportion'.

'A Black Cloud Gathers . . .'

PAGE **164** | 'dhama'—A small basket, used to measure/scoop up grain.

A List of Sources

'Ruku Dewan': First published in *Ei Somoy*, 2009.

'Kafan-nama': First published in *Anandabazar Patrika*, 2005.

'The Open-Winged Scorpion': 'Danamela Brishchik', first published in *Rabibasoriya Desh*, 1992.

'The Other Quilt': 'Onyo Nakshi', first published in *Sharadiya Desh*, 1986.

'Night Kohl': 'Nishi-Kajol', first published in *Little Magazine*, 1986.

'The Road': 'Path', first published in *Desh*, 1994.

'The Measure of Land': 'Jomi Jiret', first published in *Uralpool*, 2009.

'Simar': First published in *Sharadiya Ekkhan*, 1984.

'Sister': 'Bon', first published in *Robbar Pratidin*, 2007.

'A Black Cloud Gathers . . .' :'Kalo Megh Jeno Sajilo Rey', first published in *Desh*, 1996.

Translator's Acknowledgements

Translating Abul Bashar's work was not easy. The ruthlessness and lyricality of his prose, the puzzling non-linear shifts from one sentence to another, remained a constant challenge. How to translate a world, unfamiliar even to most mainstream readers of Bangla, into English was the obvious anxiety. This could not be achieved if Sunandini Banerjee did not join the journey with her admirable intuition for equivalents. I am really grateful to her for her brilliant contributions. She also captured the terrifying beauty of Bashar's world with the flaming scorpion on the cover. My heartfelt thanks also to Bishan Samaddar for his constant support and hard work on this project. I thank Chandrani Chatterjee, who was there at the beginning of this project; and Sulagana Biswas who was, as always, unfailing in her encouragement to me.

I am deeply indebted to Abul Bashar for letting me intrude upon his solitude. The many afternoons that we spent discussing the art of his storytelling are interwoven in the making of this book. My special thanks to Sahana-di, Bashar's wife, for her warmth and for preparing the list of sources for me.

Thanks, Seagull Books, for choosing Bashar. Finally!